INDOOR BONSAI

■ A Beginner's Step-by-Step Guide ■

Dave Pike

CROWOOD GARDENING GUIDES

First published in 1989 by
The Crowood Press
Gipsy Lane, Swindon,
Wiltshire SN2 6DQ

Reprinted 1990

British Library Cataloguing in Publication Data
Pike, Dave
  Indoor bonsai. a beginner's step-by-step guide
  I. Bonsai. Cultivation. Manuals
  I. Title
  635.9'772

  ISBN 1 85223 254 4

Line-drawings by Claire Upsdale-Jones
All photographs by Dave Pike, using his pet Bronica SQ-A.

Thanks to The Garden of Eden for the use of the conservatory on page 13,
and to Sungro-lite for the use of the grow light, page 115.

Typeset by Chippendale Type, Otley, West Yorkshire.
Printed in and bound in Spain by Graficas Estella, S.A. (Navarra)

Contents

CHAPTER 1

Introduction

Interest in the art of growing bonsai started to gain popularity about forty years ago. In those days bonsai trees were generally imported from Japan, and consisted of hardy outdoor trees such as pine, juniper and maple. This gave rise to the popular belief that all bonsai trees had to be kept outside. Only a few bonsai students were aware of indoor bonsai.

Today, the indoor bonsai is still classed by many of the growers of hardy outdoor trees as 'ladies' trees. Also, the advanced student is unable to force the growth, as they would for the hardy bonsai, by planting the tree outside in the garden (a soil-grown tree) due to the uncertain temperature range experienced throughout the year in Great Britain. Because of its recent beginnings in the western world there is a shortage of established indoor bonsai material. In some parts of the established bonsai world, such as China and Japan, there are those indoor bonsai which have the same mature appearance as the hardy bonsai first imported into this country. During the mid 1980s, there has been a definite move towards the indoor bonsai by all bonsai growers. Interest is increasing and therefore the sales pattern of most bonsai nurseries is changing from one hundred per cent hardy bonsai to seventy per cent indoor and thirty per cent hardy.

This change is due to the fact that many people other than the enthusiastic bonsai growers are showing an interest in these small trees, seeing them as part of their living room decorations. This in some ways is a bad sign for the bonsai clubs and societies due to the fact, although it is sad to say, that most will treat the trees as decorations and will not have the time

or interest to join a club to learn more about them. Added to this, at the moment most bonsai nurseries carry a stock of indoor and hardy bonsai; but as the demand for indoor trees increases, coupled with the trend toward most bonsai clubs growing their own hardy bonsai instead of buying imported hardy trees, then less space will be given to the hardy stock. This in some ways will benefit the English potter, as there will be no dangers from frost for their wares. Over the next ten years, therefore, I predict a definite change on the bonsai front.

As in all things, there are good and bad points. Bonsai may become too commercialised, and the 'production line' bonsai may appear, which in some cases is already happening. There is the

Fig I   A hardy outdoor pine. This tree can only stay inside for two to three days at any one time.

Fig 2   Myrtle has a scented foliage – a good tree for those with poor vision.

HARDY *V.* INDOOR

My admiration for hardy bonsai is as strong as it is for indoor bonsai and to choose between the two would be an impossible task. But I do believe the hardy bonsai grower has not given the indoor tree a chance, and it would be true to say that a few of my friends who have grown bonsai for many years have little or no knowledge of the indoor bonsai.

This book is not written to challenge the hardy bonsai, but to show some of the advantages of growing indoors, and it is written with the beginner in mind.

The first thing new growers often say when they see their first bonsai display is, 'Wouldn't it look attractive in our living room', and nine times out of ten they are referring to a specimen pine, juniper or maple. Then comes the shock; if the average living room has less than seventy per cent glass, you may only keep the hardy bonsai indoors for one or two days at any one time. When they move on to see the indoor section, the remark often heard is, 'But we have seen those growing in our local garden centre.' This would have been very true five to ten years ago and, except for those trees imported from the warmer regions of America and the pomegranates from Japan, most of the indoor bonsai would have been nothing more than glorified house plants. In recent years, however, many commercial growers from all parts of the world, and in particular the Mediterranean area, have started to realise that there is a market for their hardy outdoor trees being sold as indoor trees in colder parts of the world, so much so that new methods such as chemical control by growth hormones are being tested.

THE DISABLED PERSON

The hardy bonsai has always been a good form of alternative gardening for people confined to a wheelchair, but has been inaccessible to those bedridden and confined to the house through ill

good side, however; people such as the blind, who can work with trees which have scented foliage, or the handicapped and those who may be confined indoors through ill health, are now able to enjoy the bonsai and the pleasures it brings through the tree becoming an extension of themselves. Saying this, I would not like to frighten people away from the art by suggesting that you need to understand the philosophy and doctrines of any cult or society; in fact many people will treat their bonsai simply as an added attraction to their living room and never wish to take it any further than that. There is, however, a philosophy and a form of self-discipline if a grower wishes to learn.

Fig 3   Pictures like this one, showing hardy and indoor bonsai, can be misleading and give the impression that all trees may be kept inside.

Fig 4   A palm, found in most garden centres, can be transformed into a bonsai.

Fig 5   Interesting groups bring a landscape into the house, as shown with this
serissa group.

health. The indoor bonsai has opened up a new form of indoor gardening to those people. The disabled person can simply grow colourful shrubs, or even a complete forest of trees.

WINTER DISPLAY

Other than the conifer type, most hardy bonsai lose some of their attractiveness during the winter months. There are, however, a few hardy bonsai, such as the zelkova, which produce fine branch work and can look more authentic during the winter without leaves. On the other hand, most of the indoor bonsai tend to be evergreen trees, such as the olive and pistachio. The pomegranate can be a mixture of both. By this I mean that although the pomegranate is basically a deciduous tree (one which drops its foliage) it will tolerate a season without dropping its leaves, for one season only. There-

fore it would be safe to say that most indoor bonsai offer an interesting display throughout the year.

WEATHER CONDITIONS

It is obvious that weather conditions will not affect the indoor bonsai as much as they will the hardy outdoor bonsai, but saying that there are a few points to remember for the indoor bonsai during the winter months.

Most people will automatically place their tree on the windowsill, the obvious placement for maximum light. This is ideal during the summer, providing the tree is not in direct sunlight, but during the winter months this position will need re-thinking. The problem comes when temperatures fall below 10°C (50°F) and the curtains are drawn, isolating the tree from the living room and, therefore, the room temperature.

Fig 6   The most dangerous position for any bonsai is on top of the television or close to forms of direct heat, as shown by the indoor pine above.

Fig 7   One way of keeping the atmosphere humid around the bonsai foliage is to use a humidity tray. This also helps to control red spider mite.

Fig 8(a)   A flowering pomegranate will make an excellent indoor bonsai.

Fig 8(b)   A pomegranate landscape.

Fig 9   Although this maple has delicate foliage, it is totally unsuitable for growing in a living room.

You may say, 'but we have central heating and double-glazing.' Believe me, the temperature will still fall around the tree if it is isolated from the rest of the room. Therefore a second winter placement should be created, away from direct forms of heat. Do not place it on top of the television, radiator, near an open fire or heating fan. Gas central heating, the warm air type, will cause the biggest problem, mainly because of its dryness. Therefore, if warm air heating is used you will need to either spray the foliage with a mist gun or use a humidity tray as described earlier in the book (*see* page 10). Never allow the bottom of the pot to stand in water; always place the pot on some form of block, as shown in Fig 7.

Never forget that both indoor and hardy bonsai are living forms of art, and therefore the indoor bonsai can take its place alongside the hardy bonsai. For those who wish to follow the authentic pathway, this is still possible with indoor bonsai. Those who have been trained in the Japanese styles are reluctant to use trees and styles from other parts of the world, but I am sure the Japanese would agree that the art of bonsai, along with all other forms of art, has no boundaries or limitations except one's own ideas.

CHAPTER 2

Buying a Bonsai

Although this book is written for those who wish to grow their own bonsai from seed or cutting, there is nothing to stop you from purchasing a mature or partly trained bonsai to admire whilst developing your own bonsai. Having said that, the beginner will be faced with problems which seem to plague the bonsai world when purchasing a bonsai for the first time, and to explain these problems fully I will need to mention the outdoor as well as the indoor bonsai. At almost every show I attend I hear the same comments 'I had one but it died', 'they take too much looking after', 'good grief, look at the price of those trees.' Buying a bonsai may appear to be a difficult choice, and perhaps an expensive one,

when the beginner first starts to investigate the subject, but let us take a closer look at a few of the general problems.

'I HAD ONE BUT IT DIED'

A large section of first-time buyers have no idea how to look after a bonsai, and do not realise there are indoor and outdoor trees, and in most cases that the death is caused by placing a hardy outdoor tree inside, i.e. in the living room, and nine times out of ten on top of the television. Therefore the person purchasing the tree should ask the trader if it is an indoor or an outdoor tree, and the trader must be honest

Fig 10   The zelkova group are deciduous trees and therefore totally unsuitable for indoor growing.

Fig 11   A maple starting to enter its dormant season.

Fig 12   These are the only conditions in which a hardy bonsai may be grown indoors. Basically, it is a glorified glasshouse with large, open areas for ventilation and temperature control. Note the material on the ceiling used to diffuse strong sunlight.

with the buyer and explain the terms indoor and outdoor before advising which type of tree would be most suitable. This does not mean that no hardy bonsai will grow in household conditions, but the conditions a hardy tree will tolerate for a short period of time are very large glass areas, such as a conservatory, with plenty of light and good ventilation. Even then the hardy tree will still need a rest period during the winter months.

You the purchaser, providing you always ask for a receipt with the name of the bonsai and stating whether it is an indoor or outdoor tree, have the law on your side with this problem. If you are sold an 'indoor bonsai' which is in fact a hardy outdoor bonsai, without being told the temperature control, the need for ventilation, plus feeding, watering and winter placement, you are quite within your rights to return the tree and ask for a replacement which suits your needs, or a refund of your money. Some traders may use the terms 'hardy' or 'half-hardy'. Hardy means as it suggests, a hardy tree or shrub suitable for growing outside, and half-hardy relates to those trees or shrubs which may be placed outside during the summer, but could quite easily be destroyed by frost and low temperatures and will therefore need winter protection.

Do not fall into the trap of buying a tree having been told that the person who looks after the bonsai section has a day off or is out for their dinner break. It is always advisable to purchase a tree only when there is someone to give you sound advice. If not, then ask the trader for an information sheet, which is given to the trader by the bonsai wholesaler, or produced by the trader, and remember to make sure you have the name of the tree so you may check either with your own gardening book or by visiting your local library to see if the tree is suitable to be kept indoors (half-hardy) or outdoor (hardy). If no information is forthcoming, think again before making a purchase.

ADVICE

An information sheet should explain the conditions the bonsai will need to stay healthy. Some traders offer further support, such as a telephone information link and a customer back-up service.

If a holiday care service is offered by the trader, make sure that he has insurance to cover trees if stolen. The trader should have the right to check trees for pest and disease problems and reject those which may cause problems to other trees.

'THEY TAKE TOO MUCH LOOKING AFTER'

This is true to some extent; bonsai cannot be treated as normal house plants, they will need watering more often because of their superior pots, drainage system and compost compared to that of a house plant. I have come across traders using pots which are glazed on the inside. They very often have no idea of forming a drainage system and will use the first bag of compost found on the garden centre shelf. In some cases, even soil taken from the garden containing weeds, pests and untold diseases has been found in bonsai.

Fig 13   Pots which are glazed on the inside, such as the one shown in this photograph, are unsuitable for bonsai growing.

Purchasing trees from such traders, the first-time buyer will have plenty of work. For example, the soil or compost may dry out too quickly or become waterlogged, you may have to constantly weed the top of the pot, and in some cases try to remove the large tap root of a dandelion from the tree's root system. Feeding is also very important, and should be carried out at least once a month (*see* Chapter 4).

Therefore, to answer the question, 'do they need a lot of looking after?' I would say, a little, but often.

'GOOD GRIEF, LOOK AT THE PRICE'

It is true to say that good bonsai are never cheap, but if you look at other commercial enterprises such as the car servicing and repair trade, general house repairs and so on, their hourly rate can be far more than a five- to seven-year-old bonsai's total cost. Stop and think how much you would charge for seven years' work. From a good grower, you will find that there is a style which looks the same in each tree, but no two trees will be completely the same. In other words, a good bonsai is not produced on a conveyor belt system, and this adds to the basic price, because of the individual attention shown to each tree.

PRICE AND AGE

This can be a very difficult question mainly because the grower may start counting the age from when the seed was sown, and some seeds can take up to two years to germinate. There-fore a seed which has germinated and then grown on for five years as a bonsai from the seedling stage is in fact seven years old in working terms. This seems to be fair, because the grower has had to apply time and money throughout those two years and therefore will look for some return on the investment. Price

can also be governed by who grows the tree. A tree from a well-known grower, which has been used to illustrate books or articles, may cost as much as one hundred pounds for a ten-year-old tree. The exception to this is soil-grown trees such as Chinese water elms which grow faster and produce a thicker trunk in a short space of time. These are sometimes sold as fifty-year-old trees, but in fact have taken only five to ten years to produce. Here the trader should state whether the tree is soil- or pot-grown, although the buyer may still pay the high price, for artistic beauty rather than age in this case. In fact there are many bonsai centres already selling starter trees this way, and the good ones inform buyers that they are soil-grown trees. This is not such a big problem with the indoor bonsai, mainly due to the fact that most will not tolerate the low temperatures if grown outside in this country in an open soil area.

In real terms, the bonsai should only be classed as a bonsai seedling up to the age of five years. After this period, when the seedling is responding to the training, you can call it a bonsai, and even then it is only a beginner's bonsai. Only when it has reached the age of a similar tree reaching maturity in the wild, which could be anything from twenty-five to several hundreds of years, can you truly call it a mature bonsai. In most cases there is no way of telling the true age of a bonsai, particularly for those which are grown in soil. The signs to look for with soil-grown trees are the large pruning scars found at the top, and in some cases the side, of the tree, where it has been allowed to grow between three to five feet tall and then cut back hard as shown in Fig 14. Even those with large, thick roots grown over rock may have tell-tale signs of root grafting (where thicker roots are grafted on to the base of the tree and then covered in either tin foil or buried in soil until the graft has taken). You can also look at the inside of the tree after it has died to gain an approximate age. Therefore, to purchase a true bonsai with a history may cost several thousand pounds.

Fig 14   Large scars at the top of the trunk are tell-tale signs of a tree which has been grown in the soil, and although it may look forty to fifty years old, it may only be ten to fifteen.

Fig 15   Avoid trees which have unsightly wire marks (wire should only remain on a branch for one growing season).

IMPORTED TREES

Most bonsai centres which do not grow their own bonsai import from different parts of the world, and along with the shipment are papers giving the tree's approximate age. It is therefore down to the supplier's trustworthiness to pass on such information to the bonsai centre, which in turn passes it on to you, who must rely on the good reputation of the bonsai centre not to make any alterations.

WIRE MARKS

Check the tree for wire marks or pieces of wire embedded in its branches and reject those which show signs of serious damage. First-time buyers are often told that the marks will grow out. This is true in some cases, but I have seen trees ten years later with the wire marks still spoiling the appearance of the branches and top section of the tree.

I think that it is fair to point out at this stage that most bonsai centres which do not grow their own trees and import them, do not have the control over wiring damage, and rely on

their suppliers in other parts of the world to provide them with good, undamaged stock. It is sad to say this is not always the case. Once the shipment of trees has reached its destination it is a very costly and time-consuming process trying to send them back.

PESTS AND DISEASES

Before purchasing your bonsai, check for signs of pest and disease which, if found, should be pointed out to the trader. Most pests are quite easy to see with the naked eye, but some diseases can only be seen through microscopes or by removing parts of the tree and looking inside. As a general rule, select a plant that looks healthy, that has rich green leaves and not a dull yellow, unless the leaves are a natural yellow, are variegated, or it is approaching the autumn season. Avoid those which have rusty-looking black or brown marks on the foliage, crossing and rubbing branches, branches that are dying or showing signs of die-back.

Do not let these problems put you off, however, as there are excellent bonsai centres offering advice and guidance in purchasing a bonsai.

IMPORTANT POINTS TO REMEMBER

There is no such thing as a genetic bonsai, which will grow into the shapes and styles found in bonsai without specialised training. The seed is the same as any other seed and it should therefore be stated on the box or packet, 'These tree seeds are suitable for growing bonsai trees.' The pictures shown on the side of the box can be misleading, showing beautiful specimen pine trees, when most are grafted and, if grown from seed, would take a considerable amount of time to achieve, and at a selling price that few could afford.

The same applies to cuttings advertised for sale. Customers should be advised that, without training, the cutting will grow into a full-size tree or shrub. To omit such advice may lead the trader into trouble with the trading laws.

POTS

A true bonsai pot is designed to suit the requirements of the bonsai tree. When purchasing your bonsai, make sure that the pot meets these requirements and has the following features:

1 Make sure that the pot contains a drainage hole, or holes depending on the size of the pot. Sometimes small holes can be seen. These are for tying the tree into its pot.
2 The pot may be glazed on the outside but not on the inside of the pot (see Figs 16 and 17). Remove a small portion of compost from the edge of the pot and check to see if it is glazed. If so, reject the tree or ask the trader to change the pot.
3 Check for roots growing through the bottom of the pot. If there are any showing, the tree will need root pruning. Therefore, ask the trader to root prune (if it is the right time of year) or obtain a written undertaking stating that the trader will root prune at the correct time of year free of charge. If the trader is unwilling to do this, reject the tree and choose another one.

English Pots

There are only a few people in England who are trained potters as well as bonsai lovers, and this

Fig 16   English bonsai pots. The juniper in the cascade pot is not suitable for indoor growing.

Fig 17   Pots suitable for a tree with a cascade style.

Fig 18   Serissa with ornaments.

shows in the way they understand the needs of the bonsai grower and produce bonsai pots to suit those needs. One such English pot producer is Dave Jones from Walsall who makes a wide range of bonsai pots, trays and dishes as shown in Fig 16.

The pots are made from stoneware clay that comprises 45 per cent fine grog, a term used for previously fired clay which helps to reduce shrinkage and warpage. Pots are produced using two different processes. The first is to cover a plastic mould to form the basic bowl shape, then at a later stage the holes, legs and rims are added to the pot. The second process, the 'slab' pot, is when the clay is rolled and left to stiffen for at least a day. When the clay becomes 'leather hard', the walls, base and feet are cut and assembled. Pots such as the cascade pot have nine pieces, ten if a dragon is added to the side of the pot. The dragons are 'sprigged', a term Dave uses for clay moulded into a plaster negative and when stiffened slightly is taken out and joined to the main body of the pot.

When in their final shapes the pots are then fired twice. The first is to a temperature of 1,000°C, leaving the clay porous to absorb the glaze. The next stage is the decorating. This is where the outside of the pot is dipped into a glaze, but for those pots which have dragons, the dragon is first covered with metal oxides and then with a wax, a process known as 'wax resist'. The second firing then takes place at a temperature of 1,270°C. It is this high temperature (stoneware) firing that vitrifies the clay and ensures the pots are

frost proof, making them suitable for both indoor and outdoor bonsai.

IMPORTING BONSAI

Importing can only be carried out by a trader or individual who has acquired an import licence from the Ministry of Agriculture, Fisheries and Food. To avoid this in any way will lead to serious trouble with the authorities, but even more important than that are the problems you may cause to your own collection through introducing an unknown strain of pest or disease which could wipe out your entire collection, plus houseplants and plants growing in your garden. This may seem a bit dramatic, but take a look at the aphid. If you continue to use the same spray throughout the growing season you will find that the aphid becomes immune to the spray. Imagine trying to find a suitable new chemical to control aphids introduced from foreign countries, adding yet more to the wide range of pesticides now available.

Only a few times have I witnessed the burning of a mature bonsai imported with a pest or disease problem, and believe me, it is a sad sight to see but in most cases the only way to remedy the problem. So remember, it could be your whole collection which is burnt if you disobey the law which is put there to safeguard not only bonsai growers but also the horticultural and agricultural industry as a whole.

CHAPTER 3

Soil

The first step to growing a bonsai is to understand a little about the growing medium used and the feeds which are then applied to the made up soil. This may seem technical to some, but the soil and feeding is the 'life-blood' of a tree, and therefore it is very important to find the right balance to produce a healthy bonsai. I have chosen all the materials used in making the soils, or 'compost' as they will be termed throughout the book, from ready-made commercial material. This will avoid the confusion and drawn-out process of sterilising garden soil and leaf mould.

The soil used for growing your bonsai is unlike the normal house plant compost, which is basically peat and sand and therefore far too light to hold the tree in its pot. The compost we are looking for should be the loam type, and an open compost that allows air and water to pass

through freely, but at the same time have adequate water retention. This means your compost should have a balance of loam to give it the body, peat to hold the water and sand to help drainage, assisting the air passage through the compost and generally helping with the physical condition of the particles when placed together.

Fig 19 shows how soil particles look in an open soil. Note the large spaces in between each particle which allow air and water to pass freely through the compost. The large particle to the

moisture film   soil particle   air space

Fig 19   Soil particle, showing the film of water around it, and the structure of a good compost – air spaces are vital.

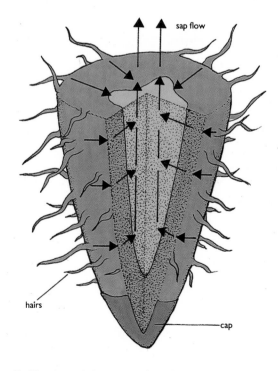

Fig 20   A root hair greatly enlarged.

Fig 21   Serissa landscape

left shows the film of water around the particle. This is where the tree starts to take in moisture through its root hairs.

The air spaces play a very important part in the health of the tree, more so with the indoor bonsai than the hardy outdoor. This is because the movement of air around the indoor bonsai is far less than the air flow around the outdoor bonsai, and therefore ventilation is an especially important factor in indoor growing. Standing the bonsai in a tray of water is not such a good idea as one might think, although this practice has been applied to many house plants over a great number of years. Many problems can arise if the holes at the bottom of the pot are blocked and the drainage and the air flow hindered. Stagnant water held in the film around the soil particles can give off toxic fumes and cause the roots to rot, for instance. Therefore, as shown in Fig 7 (page 10), always raise the pot above the water level when using a humidity tray.

Always water from the top of the pot, and only in extreme cases of dryness (which should never really be allowed to happen) will the tree need watering by capillary action.

Capillary action, or the rise of water from the bottom of the pot to the top of the pot, is an ideal way of watering very fine seeds, but a practice I prefer not to use when watering bonsai.

The compost used for bonsai should be free from weeds, pests and diseases. Soil taken from the garden should not be used unless partially sterilised first to avoid these problems. Another reason for not using garden soil is that it may contain toxic waste, such as weedkiller which has seeped out from the lawn by capillary action.

STERILISING

Sterilised soil would in reality mean a barren soil, totally without life and completely unsuitable for a tree's existence. Partially sterilising a soil by heat or chemical will free the soil from harmful organisms only, but by using a compost contain-

ing loam you will save the time and expense of partially sterilising your garden soil.

SAND

The sand used in our bonsai compost, which may also be purchased as sand and gravel, must be free of lime. Never use builders' sand or gravel (the type used in mixing cement), as it has a high lime content which will upset the pH balance and may also form a solid mass. Therefore, always buy your sand and gravel from a garden centre or garden supplies department, and make sure that it reads 'washed horticultural' sand or gravel.

LOAM/LOAMLESS

I have already mentioned the term 'loam'. Most composts sold in garden centres are loam-free, that is to say they contain peat and plant nutrients. They are much lighter and do not have the same body as a compost with loam. For this

Fig 22   Beech leaves make excellent raw material for composting.

reason they are not suitable for bonsai. With a compost that contains loam you have the heaviness to hold the tree in its pot whereas a tree in a loamless compost would need wiring into its pot.

LOAM

To produce a loam, turf is stacked upside-down in layers with decomposed straw or animal bedding lying between each layer. Loam produced by this method takes about six to seven months, which is a long and costly process and one of the reasons why there are so many loamless composts on the market.

Before trying to make your own loam, remember that it takes a long time and you will need to add lime to balance the pH to about 6.3, plus the fact that it will need sterilising. Therefore, it is far better to purchase one of the composts containing loam from your local garden centre as a starting base to your compost.

COMPOST

The materials used in making one of the composts containing loam are peat, sand, and loam which has been sterilised so that it is free from pests and diseases, to which a balance of plant nutrients are then added. A ready-made compost used on its own would not be suitable for bonsai. Later in the book you will see that some trees like an open, sandy compost and some do not. The compost purchased should only be used as a base to which more sand or peat is then added.

In some of the bags purchased from your garden centre you may find wood, paper and stones, which must be removed by sieving before using the compost. Each bag of compost will display a number from one to three, plus one marked for seed. The higher the number, the greater the fertiliser content, and the higher numbers are mainly intended to be used when up-grading a potted plant from seedling to mature plant. Thus, seed compost is for seed, number one for seedlings, up to number three for a mature plant. Through my own studies I have obtained the best results from using a seed compost followed by a foliage feed and then adding more feed at a later stage (*see* page 27).

LEAF MOULD

Leaves are broken down through composting (stacking in layers and allowing them to rot down to form a humus which looks like a black tar) and sometimes added to a bonsai compost to give it more body. Depending on the type of leaves used, this will vary in its quality. I have found that leaves from hawthorn and beech are the best. If you do add leaf mould to your compost, make sure it has been partially sterilised before using it, to remove pests, diseases and weeds. (Never use leaves that show signs of disease.)

PEAT

There are two types of peat – moss peat, which is light brown in colour and looks like flakes of tobacco, and sedge peat which appears black and sooty in texture and can turn to a dust when dry. Always use the moss peat; it will cost more but has the heaviness and the body we need in our bonsai compost.

COMPOST MIXTURES

There are five types of compost: seed, cuttings, seedlings, light sandy, and heavy. Fresh compost containing loam should be purchased from your local garden centre. To prepare it, mix in the ratios shown under each section as follows:

Code 1: Seed Compost
80% seed compost, 10% moss peat, 10% sharp sand.

23

There are also different forms of volcanic substances available from local garden centres which are suitable for seed growing.

Code 2: Cutting Compost
50% moss peat and 50% sharp sand.
As with seed compost, there are forms of volcanic substances suitable for taking cuttings.

Code 3: Open, Sandy Compost
60% seed compost containing loam, 20% moss peat and 20% sharp sand.

Code 4: Medium Compost
70% seed compost containing loam, 15% moss peat and 15% sharp sand.

Code 5: Heavy Compost
80% seed compost containing loam, 10% moss peat and 10% sharp sand.

COMPOST MIXING

The area where you mix your compost must be clean. This can be a large wooden board or a clean area of concrete. Measure your materials of moss peat, sand, compost containing loam and leaf mould (if used) and place them in a pile next to each other on your clean surface. Start by mixing and sieving the compost using a 1.5mm sieve to remove very fine particles, keeping any particles over this size, followed by the moss peat which should be graded with a 5mm sieve. Mix these two materials together and sieve the combined mixture once more through a 1.5mm sieve. Sand should then be added to the compost and peat. When all three materials are in one heap, turn the heap three times allowing the materials to form a compost with a combination of large and small particles. If the materials are too dry, water may be applied in small amounts when mixing, but only to counteract the dust. At the end of the mixing you should have a compost that feels gritty, but at the same time silky when flowing through your fingers.

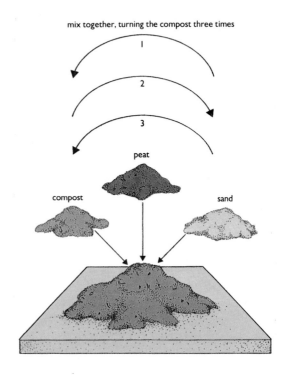

Fig 23 Mixing compost. This should always be done on a clean surface.

FEEDING

Feeding is a very important factor when growing a bonsai, and even more so with the indoor bonsai. Although we are trying to slow down the rate of growth on our tree, in real terms we are only talking of height, and therefore we are still looking to produce a thick trunk, followed by branches which are proportionately balanced to the thickness of that trunk and a strong, healthy, fibrous root system. Essential nutrients which help to produce such a healthy, well-balanced growth and resist diseases are fed to the tree throughout its growing season.

These essential nutrients are divided into two types; major elements and trace elements.

Major Elements

The first three major elements are what I term 'invisible' elements. By this I mean they cannot be found on the feeding packets at garden centres. They are carbon, hydrogen and oxygen. Carbon is found in the air which passes through the compost and around the tree. Hydrogen can be found in the water which is applied to the compost daily during the growing season, and oxygen is found both in water and air. Therefore, by providing the bonsai with a compost which allows air to pass freely around the soil particles, together with the water, you are adding the first of the three major elements.

N:P:K (nitrogen, phosphorus and potassium), also major elements, are applied by feeding.

Nitrogen

The bonsai tree will use nitrogen for most of its major growth processes, such as growing the stem and leaves, and it helps to give the tree its green colour by assisting in the formation of chlorophyll (the green colouring matter found in plants). Care should be taken not to over-feed your bonsai with nitrogen, for fear of producing weak, sappy growth which could be damaged by cold weather, strong winds and pests.

Phosphorus

This plays an important role in the formation of cells in the young bonsai, particularly in root formation. It may seem strange to encourage the roots to grow when most of the time we are trying to control them, but it is very important that the tree maintains a good, strong, healthy root system, to help it through its strenuous training programme during the coming seasons.

Potassium

This will help your bonsai through the cold winter spells, by controlling sap movement and building up the tree's resistance to disease.

N:P:K are widely known by most bonsai growers as major elements. However, there are three others which also play their part in the health of your bonsai tree and these are as follows:

Calcium

This also helps in the formation of cells, and strengthens the tree's structure, developing the growing tips of the tree and its roots.

Magnesium

As with nitrogen, magnesium helps to form chlorophyll and works with phosphorus, which in turn assists in seed formation. One of the main causes of yellow leaves is magnesium deficiency, a term which we call 'chlorosis'.

Sulphur

This is used in protein formation and helps the production of oils in the tree.

Trace Elements

The bonsai tree will only require small amounts of trace elements, such as iron, copper, boron, zinc, manganese and molybdenum. These trace elements work closely with other major elements by speeding up the chemical reaction taking place inside the tree.

Iron and Manganese

Both help with the formation of chlorophyll, and a deficiency will cause yellowing of leaves (chlorosis).

Boron

This works with calcium, which strengthens the tree's structure, and a deficiency will hinder disease protection.

Fig 24   Serissa, rocks and a Chinese figure make an interesting landscape.

All of the chemical fertilisers used should contain major and trace elements. Be sure to read the packet when purchasing from your local garden centre.

FEEDING CHANGES

In the list below I give three feeding changes to be made through the growing season, for spring, summer and autumn. By using and combining them with the compost which is low in nutrients

it will give you more control over the growth rate during the growing season.

Two Forms of Feeding

Plant food can generally be found in two forms:

1 Foliage feed; a balance of nutrients enter through the foliage.
2 Powder or granule; apply with water when watering.

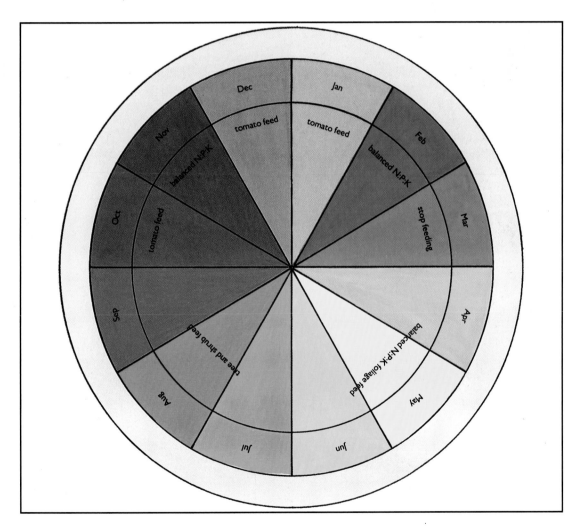

Fig 25   Feeding clock for the bonsai year.

Over-Feeding

Without becoming too technical, understanding the way the plant takes in its water and nutrients (salts), will make you more aware of over-feeding. If you place a spoonful of sugar on the surface of a cup of tea and allow the tea to slowly spread throughout the sugar, you will see, in a simple way, how the bonsai takes water and salts into its cell system through a selectively permeable membrane, by osmosis.

When the cell can no longer take in water, or in other words is full, creating an outward pressure on the wall of the cell, we say that the cell is turgid.

Plasmolysis

If the solution around the soil particle is more concentrated than the cell sap due to over-feeding, the cell allows water to pass out by exosmosis which in turn pulls the cytoplasm away from the cell wall, causing the cell to shrink, or become flaccid. This is one of the main causes of wilting. Therefore, always follow a feeding programme closely; it may be more helpful if the beginner keeps the dilution rate slightly under the recommended level.

IMPORTANT   Always read the instructions given on the box, bottle, or packet. Never over-feed your tree. If the growth is too slow and you are working to a feeding programme, do not be tempted to add more feed as this can result in root damage and soil contamination. Always use a clean watering-can or sprayer, never use the same container for which you would use weed-killer, insecticide, or cleaning fluid. Finally, always wash out your container after feeding, then wash your hands with clean water.

ORGANIC FEED

'Organic Feed' or to give it its full title, 'Concentrated Organic Manure', is a produce from animal and plant residues and therefore should not be classed as organic feed until such time as it has decomposed after being mixed with a compost.

Many new bonsai growers will come across the advanced students who, when mixing their compost, add organic manures such as hoof and horn, dried blood and bone meal. It is not easy to use these organic feeds, and is totally different to feeding a large, open area of soil in the garden. Untold damage may result through the compost

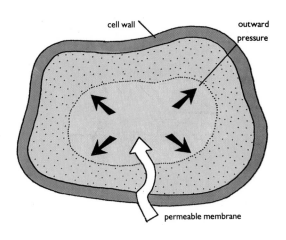

Fig 26 (a)   A cell which is full of water is known as a 'turgid' cell.

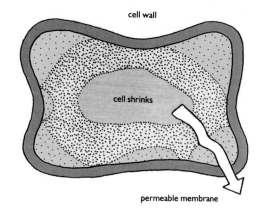

Fig 26 (b)   A flaccid cell. Cells may collapse in this way through over-feeding.

becoming toxic, and therefore the beginner should follow this basic set of rules:

1   Always ask to see the advanced student's tree that has been planted in such compost, then if the tree looks healthy, take this advanced student's tips (if the person is willing to pass them on) and practise on old material first.
2   Always make sure that the organic substances are the current year's stock and that they are in a dry condition before use.
3   Read through the following list of organic substances before attempting to use them and try to work out the amounts of nitrogen, phosphates and potash you are giving to the compost, and remember the amounts of N:P:K already in the compost you are adding to (unless using a compost totally free of plant nutrients).

Organic Substances

Hoof and Horn

Mainly nitrogen, between 7 per cent and 15 per cent, with far less amounts of phosphorus acid. When added to a standard potting compost without being completely free of nutrients, the rate applied is 1.25 kg per cubic metre.

Dried Blood

Dried blood is a quick-acting organic feed containing 7 to 14 per cent nitrogen with 1 to 2 per cent phosphoric acid. It is mainly applied as a top dressing (placed on top of the compost surface) at 17 to 34 grams per square metre. This may be a problem to those of you who are not too good at mathematics. Therefore, to calculate the amount for your bonsai, mark a piece of card dividing the surface area of the square metre into equal sections, then divide by weight the dried blood into equal amounts for each section. Now place your bonsai tree on to the marked card and apply the top dressing. At first, the beginner should apply the dressing slightly under the rate shown above.

Fish Guano

After the oil has been extracted from the fish it is then dried and ground down to produce a powder containing approximately equal amounts of between 6 to 9 per cent nitrogen and 6 to 9 per cent phosphoric acid. This produces a balanced feed containing the important N and P which is fast-acting as well as long-lasting. The older Japanese practices of feeding would have used this form of organic food which they term fish meal. The only problem is the lack of potash (K), but if you read on, wood ash will provide this third important ingredient.

Wood Ash

Wood ash is produced by burning clean, healthy branches. This ash is rich in mineral salts, the most important being potash, and the level is between 1 to 7 per cent, which is then applied at the rate of 135 to 270 grams per square metre. Because of its soluble state the salts are very fast-acting. However, there are certain rules which should be followed before attempting to manufacture your own wood ash.

1   For young bonsai growers I would strongly recommend that an adult supervises the burning of the wood.
2   Never add petrol, paraffin or rubber tyres to the fire. In fact the fire should be totally free from man-made objects such as wire and plastic, with paper being the exception to the rule. Clean paper should be the only form of lighting material.
3   Make sure the fire is contained in an area away from objects which may explode or catch fire. If possible build a fire area similar to a barbecue with fire bricks.
4   Allow the fire area to cool down before attempting to collect the ash.
5   Store the ash in a clean, dry area away from small children and pets.

Fig 27   Five pomegranates in a Dave Jones pot.

Unsuitable Organic Feeds

Bone Meal

Bone meal is not the most practical of organic feeds to use for growing bonsai, basically because it is a very slow-acting form of phosphoric acid feed containing 20–25 per cent phosphoric acid and smaller amounts of nitrogen (approximately 3–4 per cent). The problem for the bonsai grower is mixing the bone meal far enough in advance to allow time for it to break down ready for the tree to take in the phosphoric acid. If added to a compost at a very early stage and allowed to stand for several months, it would be totally unsuitable as the compost may have become too toxic through the reaction of the different feeds mixing together and not being used. It would, therefore, be far better to find alternative forms of phosphoric acid through a normal packet feed containing N:P:K plus trace elements.

Poultry Manure

This form of feed, if given when fresh, will seriously damage the fine fibrous root system of the bonsai. Although it is high in nitrogen and phosphoric acid, I would advise the beginner and also the advanced student against its use unless a careful study has been carried out into the effect this feed will have on the tree's growth.

Farmyard Manure

Farmyard manure (FYM) is used as a soil conditioner for outside growing areas, rather than a form of feed, because of its low N:P:K content. On testing a small sample, it was found to contain:

N   0·4–0·6 per cent
P   0·2–0·3 per cent
K   0·5–0·7 per cent

I would advise the beginner and the advanced bonsai student to leave this type of feed out of your bonsai practice.

CHAPTER 4

Growing Indoor Bonsai

Indoor bonsai is fairly new to the bonsai scene, and therefore it is harder to find young seedling material for indoor than it is for hardy outdoor bonsai (which can be found at most good garden centres and nurseries). It is very doubtful whether such indoor material is available at your local garden centre, unless you are fortunate to live close to a nursery which specialises in house plants. Therefore, either a visit to a bonsai centre, or growing from seeds and cuttings are the only alternatives.

STOCK PLANTS

A stock plant is a plant not grown as a bonsai, but treated as a normal plant, grown in a large pot and used to produce cuttings. Once you have purchased a suitable stock plant for indoor bonsai growing, this can be used once or twice a year to produce softwood and semi-ripe cuttings as shown a little later (page 36).

SEED PACKETS

Most garden centres do not stock tree seeds, and especially not tropical tree seeds, but they do usually carry a supplier's list and are able to order them for you. Seeds such as the pomegranate can be found in most of the catalogues, but to obtain more unusual seeds you may have to write to or visit a seed specialist or bonsai centre.

SEEDS

Indoor Seeds – Temperature

Most indoor seeds will need some form of heat, and when sown in a seed tray as shown on page 34 will need placing in a propagator, heated glasshouse, warm bench or cold frame with heating cables.

Fig 28 Young pomegranate seedlings. Note the unusual-shaped seed leaves at the bottom.

Electric Propagator

For those who would like more than the odd cutting or seed packet but still on a small scale, it would be far better to purchase a small electric propagator. By controlling the growing environment you will be able to grow softwood, semi-ripe cuttings and provide the higher temperatures for some of the indoor tree seeds without too many problems. Two important components you will need on your propagator are a thermostatic control and a ventilation area. The ventilation area can be in the form of a sliding door at the front and back of the propagator, or vents on the side. Also in garden centres, you will find plastic tops which are made to fit pots and trays. These are ideal for semi-ripe cuttings from

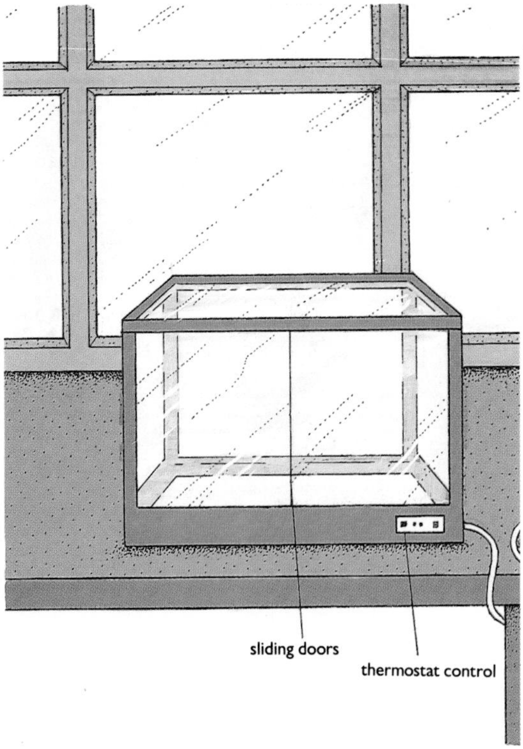

Fig 29   A simple electric propagator placed inside a glasshouse will give you more control when taking cuttings.

sliding doors

thermostat control

May to August, but they do not have the same control as an electric propagator.

Fig 29 shows an example of the type of propagating case available. Note that this has a movable opening for ventilation and access. Remember that it is electric and therefore you will also need to be close to a power point, which may be a problem because the light factor will also need to be taken into consideration. You can overcome the problem of the power point by using an extension lead, but remember never to allow the lead to come into contact with water or wet areas, and always extend the cable to its full length (not coiled), otherwise the cable may overheat and cause a fire.

The temperature for general seed sowing should be 12–18°C (54–64°F), but some of the exotic trees, such as baobab, may need a slightly higher temperature. (*See* Chapter 6.)

Warm Bench

The warm bench will need an area such as a glasshouse. As you can see in Fig 30, it is a small bench with sides and a very fine mesh (less than 4mm) covering the bottom to allow drainage. The bench should be sited over a soil or gravelled area which will allow the water to drain away from the bench. It should be covered with 6mm gravel, on top of which a thin layer of mixed sand and gravel is then spread. An electric warming cable is then placed on top in several U-shapes, with one end connected to a thermostat which controls the temperature. More sand is added on top of the cables. When plugged in, the cables heat up the sand and give bottom heat to the pots containing the cuttings.

Cold Frame

Cold frames used for taking cuttings of indoor bonsai may only be used between late spring and mid summer. They are best suited for semi-ripe cuttings or hardening off softwood cuttings taken earlier in the year. It is suitable for growing on cold room bonsai such as Chinese water elm,

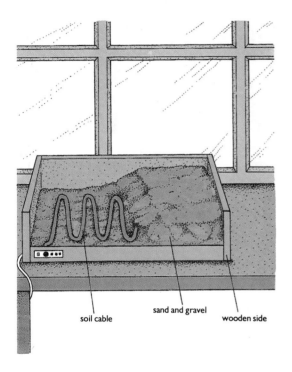

soil cable   sand and gravel   wooden side

Fig 30   A warm bench.

Fig 31   A cold frame used for hardening seedlings during late spring, or used for semi-ripe cuttings in mid-summer.

Jacqueline elm and olive trees during the summer months. There are many cold frames on the market, many of which are unfortunately of poor quality and to use such a cold frame may result in a loss of heat. The old brick or wood cold frame is hard to come by unless you are a D.I.Y. person, but it would be worth having one constructed. The type we are looking for should be well made, of brick or wood, and lined with polythene. The lid must fit securely but be easily removable to allow ventilation and hardening-off. The bottom of the cold frame will need good drainage, which can be obtained by digging a hole the same shape as the cold frame and filling it with hardcore and gravel. An electric warming cable could be fitted in the bottom, making a cold frame and a warm bench together, although this would need the advice of a qualified electrician due to the wet weather conditions that will be met outdoors.

Step one

Always use a clean seed tray, with plenty of drainage holes at the bottom.

Step two

Half-fill the seed tray with a seed compost, similar to the one described on page 23 (compost Code 1) and firm it down with a firming board, as illustrated in Fig 32. Many growers find a high degree of success by using one of the volcanic substances available from the local garden centre. If this is used it can be mixed with Code 1 compost at the rate of:

75% volcanic substance
25% compost Code 1

Fill seed tray and firm as mentioned above. Large seeds should be spaced out over the surface of the compost as shown in Fig 32, whilst small seeds can be sprinkled, spacing them as much as possible at the same time.

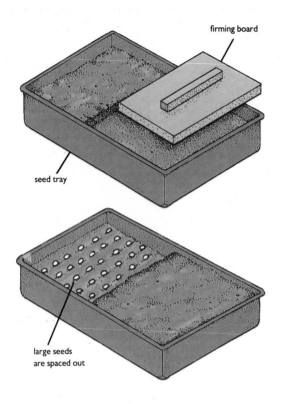

firming board

seed tray

large seeds
are spaced out

*Fig 32   Planting seeds. Do not cover very fine
seeds with compost.*

Step three

Cover the large seed with a 5–7mm ($\frac{1}{8}$–$\frac{1}{4}$in) layer of compost. The small seeds should have a fine layer, just enough to cover the seed, but very fine seeds should not be covered. In the case of seeds between large and fine, · the compost should be applied by passing it through a sieve.

Step four

Water the seeds, using a watering-can with a fine rose or capillary action for very fine seed. First start the water flow away from the tray, then move it backwards and forwards across the compost area, moving the can away from the tray before it runs out of water. By doing this you will not form puddles or holes in the compost, which would bury or wash away the seeds. When watering with capillary action for very fine seeds, check that the seeds are not pulled too deep into the soil when allowing the excess water to drain away.

Step five

When the seeds have developed their first seed leaves (cotyledon) and are large enough to handle, pot them (prick them out) into small pots, using a compost Code 4 for young seedlings (*see* page 24). Care should be taken

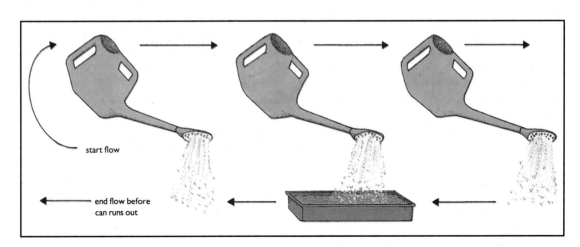

start flow

end flow before
can runs out

*Fig 33   Move the watering can backwards and forwards over the seed tray
to avoid puddling.*

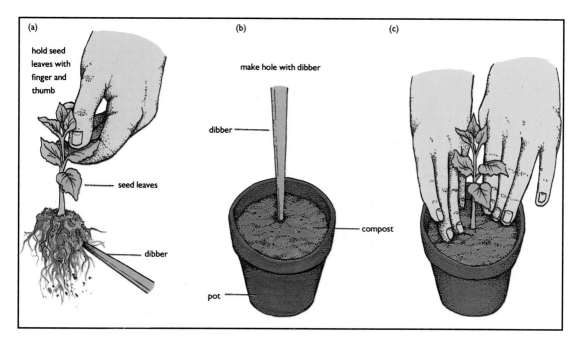

Fig 34   It is very important not to damage the stem when transplanting (pricking out) very young seedlings.

not to damage the stem when pricking out. One way to overcome the problem of damaging the stem would be to take hold of the seed leaves (the leaves which develop before true leaves), then push a dibber (an ice-lolly stick is ideal for this) into the compost a few centimetres away from the stem down to the bottom of the seed tray and under the tap root of the seedling. Lift and gently pull on the seed leaves, but do not at any time force the seedling. Seeds which develop needles (such as a Jerusalem pine, *Pinus halefecis*) do not have a seed leaf stage, and in this case you should follow the lifting process without handling the stem.

Damping Off

One of the most troublesome and probably the most common problem for the beginner when growing bonsai from seed is a soil-borne fungal disease termed 'damping off' (*Pythium* and *Rhizoctonia solani*). The stem is damaged at soil level or just above, roots may rot and you are left with a black stump covered in a grey mould, or *Botrytis cinerea* as it is technically called. The chemical control offered on the shelves of garden centres is not always effective. Copper fungicide backed by good hygiene such as clean seed trays and partially sterilised compost is the best possible prevention against the disease. As far as possible, follow the procedure outlined below:

1   Always wash seed trays with a horticultural disinfectant before using them.
2   Never use the same seed compost to sow a second batch of seeds.
3   Make sure that the tray never becomes waterlogged and try to control the level of humidity, keeping it to a minimum.
4   Spray with a copper fungicide.

Fig 35 *Young pomegranate cuttings.*

CUTTINGS

Softwood

These are cuttings taken from the current season's wood (new growth), from April to June, and to January if heat is used.

Semi-Ripe

Again, current season's wood is used; the base of this cutting should be woody, and taken between July and October.

General Rules

Collect strong, healthy side shoots. The best time for this is first thing in the morning. Place all material collected in plastic bags to stop them from drying out. Always pick non-flowering material that is free from pest and diseases.

Cutting Compost

The compost for all types of cuttings is Code 2, or use one of the volcanic substances available for cuttings. If volcanic substances are used the rate should be as follows:

50% volcanic substance
50% compost Code 2

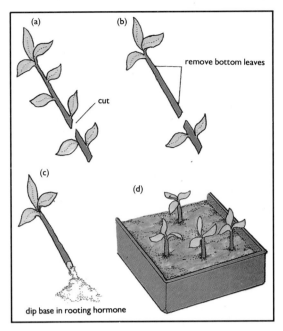

Fig 36 *Softwood cuttings taken early in the year. Never use flowering shoots for cuttings.*

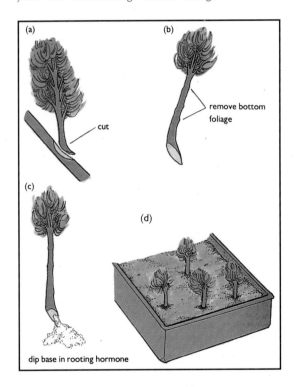

Fig 37 *Semi-ripe cuttings taken in mid-summer. Most semi-ripe cuttings will root without heat.*

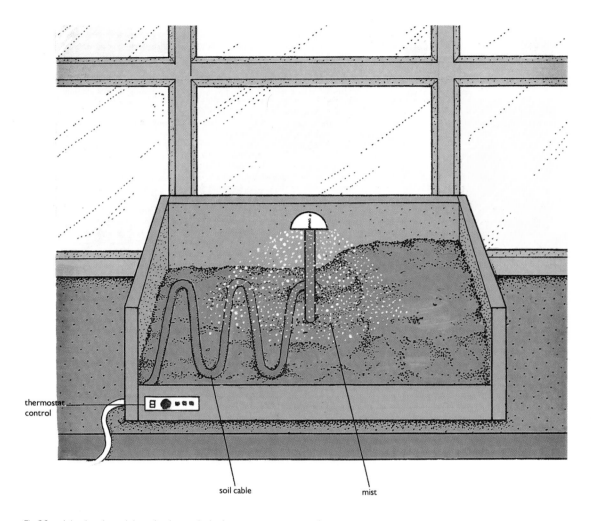

thermostat
control

soil cable   mist

Fig 38   A basic mist unit in a glasshouse is the best way to grow cuttings.

Preparation (Softwood)

Cut just below a node, *see* Fig 36. The length should be between 5cm (2in) and 7.5cm (3in). The leaves from the lower part of the cutting should be removed.

Dip the base of the cutting into a rooting hormone and push it gently into the cutting compost. Place the cutting under mist or on to a warm bench or propagator.

Mist Unit

The mist unit is a form of bench with electric warming cables running through a sand and gravel base. These cables are controlled by a thermostat and the temperature is kept around 20°C (70°F). A circuit-breaker called an 'electric leaf' is fitted, which turns the mist jets on and off, keeping the area humid. Fig 38 shows a large mist unit, but for the person who wishes only to take fifty to one hundred cuttings, there are smaller mist units which can be purchased from your local garden centre.

Aftercare

If the tips of the cuttings are starting to shoot and a white root system can be seen, this is a good sign that the cuttings have taken. Remove the cuttings from the tray and pot them individually into small pots containing one of the composts with a suitable pH, such as Code 3 or 4. Then place the pots back, at the same temperature, with an increase of the light factor for a week or two for the cutting to become established. Then harden the cuttings off by slowly lowering the temperature, giving them more air and removing them from the propagation area.

Preparation (Semi-Ripe)

The collection and preparation for semi-ripe cuttings is very similar to the softwood cutting – node cuttings – but the length is slightly longer at 5–10cm (2–4in). This is the type of cutting that can be taken during the warmer months of the year and is particularly suitable if you are unable to provide artificial heat.

Aftercare

Check for new growth and a white root system. If the cuttings have rooted, pot as for the softwood cutting. For those classed as cold room bonsai, such as the olive, and grown in a cold frame with heated cables, give them ventilation on warm days, but be careful of a sudden change in the weather conditions. Alternatively, slowly introduce them indoors into cold room conditions with plenty of light, but not direct sunlight.

TRAINING SOFTWOOD AND SEMI-RIPE CUTTINGS

Once the cuttings have taken root, move them into individual pots and place them back into the same temperature for the next week or two. After this period, move them closer to the door

if grown in a glasshouse, leave the top slightly open if grown in a cold frame. This will gradually introduce the cuttings to normal weather conditions and avoid 'shocking' them if placed outside too soon. For a small propagator, lower the temperature and allow more air to enter. This will give the seedlings a chance to acclimatise to the weather conditions outside the growing area. Pinch out the growing tips during the first year, but do not attempt to prune the root system at this stage. Check the watering every day, but do not over-water them for the first four weeks. Start feeding with a balanced foliage spray fertiliser after four weeks from repotting and then every three weeks. Spray for pests and diseases.

Air-Layering

There are three ways to air-layer. The first is generally used for house plants and is quite good for the beginner to try, the second and third are used by some of the hardy bonsai growers, but are also suitable for indoor bonsai.

Technique 1   Many bonsai are started by this process, mainly because it is possible to air-layer old wood as well as young. The young wood will root within twelve months, but older wood may take longer. The advantages with this form of propagation are that trees with a thick trunk can be produced in a short time and trees which would normally be too tall, or as we term them too 'leggy', can still be used.

The first thing you need to do is to pick a suitable branch or area just above the 'leggy' section, with the thickness of the trunk in mind, and a well-spaced network of branches. The part of the tree chosen for air-layering can be encouraged to grow in the desired shape by pruning one or two years before propagation takes place, as shown in Fig 39 (a).

Make a cut half-way through the branch or at the base of your future trunk, as shown in Fig 39 (b).

Dust the blade of your knife with a rooting

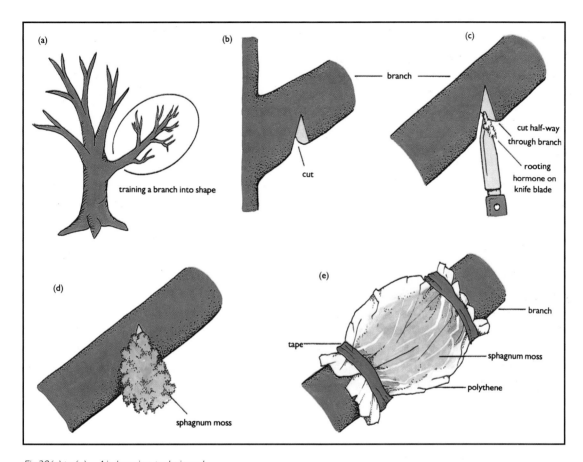

(a) training a branch into shape

(b) branch / cut

(c) branch / cut half-way through branch / rooting hormone on knife blade

(d) sphagnum moss

(e) branch / sphagnum moss / polythene / tape

Fig 39(a) to (e) Air-layering, technique 1.

hormone of the type used for semi-ripe and hardwood cuttings. Run the blade of the knife through the cut you have just made, wiping the hormone powder from the blade into the cut (*see* Fig 39 (c)). The cut is then kept open by packing moist sphagnum moss into it. More moist sphagnum moss is added outside the cut and the section of the branch is wrapped in clear polythene and sealed at both ends with tape, as shown in Fig 39 (e). When the polythene is filled with a white root growth, the air-layer can be removed from the mother tree.

Technique 2   The second way of air-layering is an old practice using copper wire (aluminium training wire could be used instead of the copper wire). The wire is wound round a section of the branch or trunk and then tightened, cutting into the bark. Moss is placed around the wound and covered. Another way to do this is to strip a complete section of the bark from around the branch or trunk. I have found that both ways will interfere with the sap flow to the area which is to become the new bonsai, or to put it another way, the mother tree cannot feed the branch whilst developing the root system. This really is an example of old practices by people who have mastered the art, and therefore I would advise the beginner to choose one of the other two ways of air-layering.

Technique 3   The third is very similar to the

39

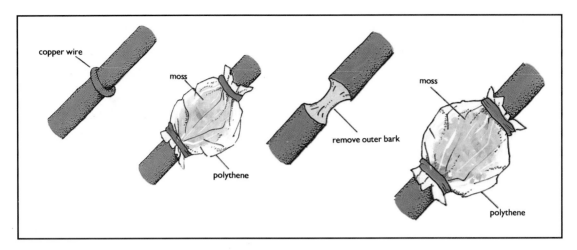

Fig 40   Air-layering, technique 2.

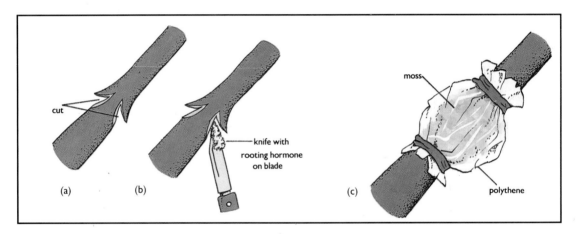

Fig 41   Air-layering, technique 3.

first method, except that two cuts are made, one each side of the trunk or branch, as illustrated in Fig 41. It is important to remember to keep the cuts open, and this is done by packing with moss peat. The area should then be covered in the same way as the first air-layer technique.

Grafting

Although I would advise the beginner to start developing bonsai skills by growing from seed, cuttings or nursery stock, it would be nice at a later stage to try a hand at grafting. Once the art has been mastered it is possible to graft a branch from one tree on to another tree of the same type but of a different flower colour, and thereby produce an attractive bonsai containing two different coloured flowers.

When grafting, the two surfaces are held firmly together using raffia, a tough string-looking material. It can also be used to cover wire if wiring a tree with a soft bark. Grafting wax helps to keep water out of the union and also stops the area from drying out. The wax is heated, then applied with a brush.

Types of Graft

There are several ways of grafting, but I shall only show two examples to grow indoor bonsai; the cleft graft and the veneer graft.

A cleft graft is a good way to produce a bonsai with a thick trunk and a network of top branches. The root-stock used for the cleft graft is much thicker than the scion or scions. A V–shape cut is made at the top of the root-stock and the scion is wedged into this cut (*see* Fig 42). The graft is then wrapped with raffia.

For a veneer graft, bottom heat is advisable. The end of the scion is shaped as in Fig 43, then placed into a cut made low down the root-stock.

The rest of the chapter is split into two years. The first year will cover the basic practices used to form the shape of your bonsai tree, such as pruning, pruning cuts and wiring, and the second year will cover the root pruning. For the remaining three years of a five-year training plan you will need to read the next chapter which explains styles and shapes in more detail. Therefore read through this chapter before attempting to form the shape you are looking for, choose shapes and follow the step-by-step guide.

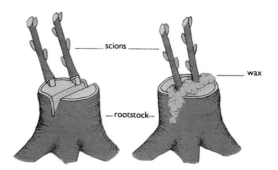

Fig 42   A cleft graft. The most important factor is to bring the cambium of the scion and root-stock into full contact

Growing from seed or cuttings will take up to five years to produce something that looks like a bonsai, but you will find that each stage from the first set of seed leaves or sign of roots will bring a fascination of its own. After the first five years you will be able to sit back and admire the fruits of your labour.

Year One

Step One (Seed)

Once the seeds have germinated, prick them out into individual pots. Care should be taken

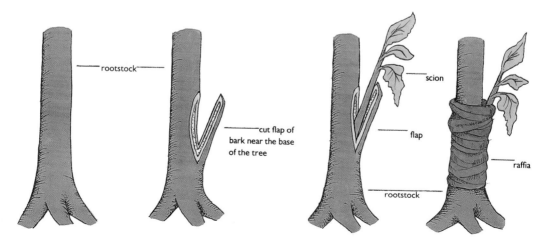

Fig 43   A veneer graft. Again the secret is to link the two cambium layers together

not to damage the young shoots and roots when removing from the compost. Try to lift the seedlings by first taking hold of one seed leaf (the leaves which develop before the true leaves) with your finger and thumb, then, being very careful not to damage the stem, lift the roots with as much compost as possible and transplant them by making a hole with a dibber, as described on page 35, into a Code 3 or 4 compost according to whether the tree likes an acid or a neutral compost. Do not prune the roots this year.

Step One (Cuttings)

Once the cuttings have taken root, remove them carefully with as much compost as possible on the root system and, without pulling them from the cutting compost system, transplant them into the compost Code 3 or 4, again depending on the type of tree.

Step Two (Seedlings from Seed and Cuttings)

Keep the room temperature between 16–18°C (61–64°F) and give the seedling as much light as possible, but not strong sunlight, turning the seedling each day to ensure that it receives light from all sides to give it a balanced growth pattern.

Watering and Feeding

Do not feed for the first two weeks after transplanting and never allow the compost to become waterlogged. After two weeks, plan a feeding programme using the fertilisers referred to at the beginning of the chapter, starting with a foliage feed. Feeding this way will allow the tree to be fed, but at the same time leave the root system free to develop its feeding hairs. Water before the compost becomes completely dry, or as a general rule every other day. Mist over the foliage if the atmosphere becomes dry, or every day where there is gas central heating, and

Fig 44   Jacqueline elm in its second year, cut back hard in March.

every other two days with other types of heating.

Feeding Programme

April to May   Foliage feeding with a N:7 P:7 K:7 plus trace elements.
June to August   Change to a fertiliser containing N:10 P:14 K:18 plus trace elements.
September to February   Use a tomato feed with trace elements.
March   Do not feed, as this is root pruning time.

Pinching, pruning, bud rubbing and wiring is the basic training for the indoor bonsai for the next five years and we term this type of training 'cosmetic'. It needs constant attention, unlike the root pruning and removal of large branches, which are normally carried out once a year. Remember, root pruning will be explained in the second year. (See page 47.)

Fig 45   The same elm as in Fig 44, six months later, showing the new growth.

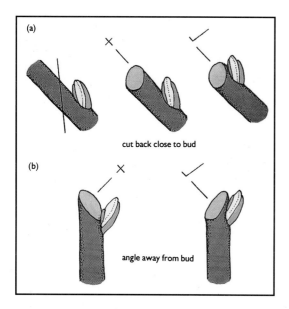

Fig 46   Cutting back to buds. (a) Prune close to a bud. (b) Angle as shown to prevent water build-up at the base of the bud.

Shaping

For the first four weeks after transplanting, either from seed or cuttings, allow the seedling to recover from the shock of its move – in other words do not worry about forming a shape. The golden rule is to remember that the health of the tree comes before its bonsai training. (*See* four basic shapes in Chapter 5.)

Pruning Cuts

When cutting back to a bud it is very important that you make a clean cut and do not leave stumps (*see* Fig 46 (a)).

Pruning Angle

The angle of the pruning cut should be made so that water will run away from the bud or pruned area, as shown in Fig 46 (b). To leave stumps or an area which will hold or direct water into the base of a bud will cause rot, die-back and disease such as coral spot. (*See* page 111 for coral spot and its treatment.)

Pruning to a Bud

Pruning to a bud is the natural way to shape your tree. First select a bud which is facing the direction in which you would like to form a branch. By cutting back to this bud you will force the new growth in that direction, as shown in Figs 46 and 47.

Wiring

Do not over-wire your tree during the first year – try to shape from buds as far as possible. If you do have to wire during the first year, make sure the branch is woody and not green and sappy,

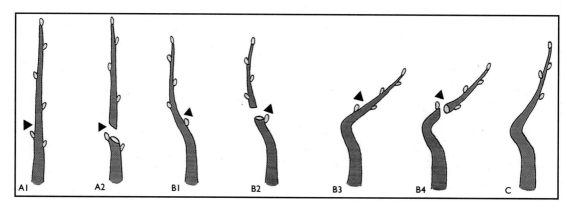

Fig 47   As far as possible, try to shape the trunk or branch from bud growth.

otherwise the wire will cut and damage the bark, leaving it open and exposed to diseases. Cover wire with raffia for all trees during the first two years.

Wiring should only be carried out if you are unable to shape the bonsai by pruning (*see above*) and the beginner should not fall into the trap of thinking that all bonsai are automatically wired. In fact bonsai wire can be very damaging if used inexpertly. The wire should not be too tightly bound, but at the same time should be secure enough to hold the branch or trunk in the position in which it has been set. At one time the only wire used for bonsai training was copper, but in modern day bonsai work, it is made of aluminium which can be purchased in several different gauges ranging from 1.0mm to 6.0mm. The two most important rules to remember when wiring are firstly never wire new, sappy growth (wait until it becomes woody), and secondly never leave the wire on for more than

one growing season. Very serious damage to the bark and permanent scarring will result if it is not removed. To give added protection to those bonsai which have soft barks, cover the wire with raffia as shown in Fig 48 (a).

Many trees imported from other countries have tell-tale signs of over-wiring; some still contain pieces of wire embedded in their bark. If the beginner should purchase such a bonsai, remove the wire as soon as possible.

Many bonsai growers, and not always the beginner, damage branches when removing wire. If the wire is cut at the points as in Fig 48 (b) it will practically fall off without damaging the branch.

Wiring the Main Trunk

Step one Bonsai seedlings between the age of one to three years old lend themselves quite readily to being shaped with wire, but it may be advisable to use a clamp for older bonsai. However, for those bonsai which have supple trunks and where the bark has started to form a woody texture, start by first cutting a length of wire slightly longer than the trunk. Push the wire into the soil as shown in Fig 49. The anchoring of the wire plays a very important part in keeping the wire firm and therefore helping to hold the position you are about to create.

Step two Working upwards, wrap the wire around the trunk as in Fig 49. The gauge of wire used depends on the thickness of the trunk.

Step three Hold the base of the tree firmly with one hand, and with the other carefully bend and twist the trunk until you reach the desired shape, as in Fig 49. Avoid covering buds, as far as possible position wire in between the bud system (Fig 49).

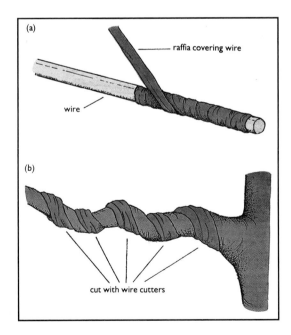

Fig 48   Wiring. (a) Raffia will help protect the bark from damage. (b) Never try to remove the wire by unwinding. Using wire cutters, cut at the points shown.

Wiring a Branch

Step one The beginner will find it easier to wire two branches at the same time rather than

45

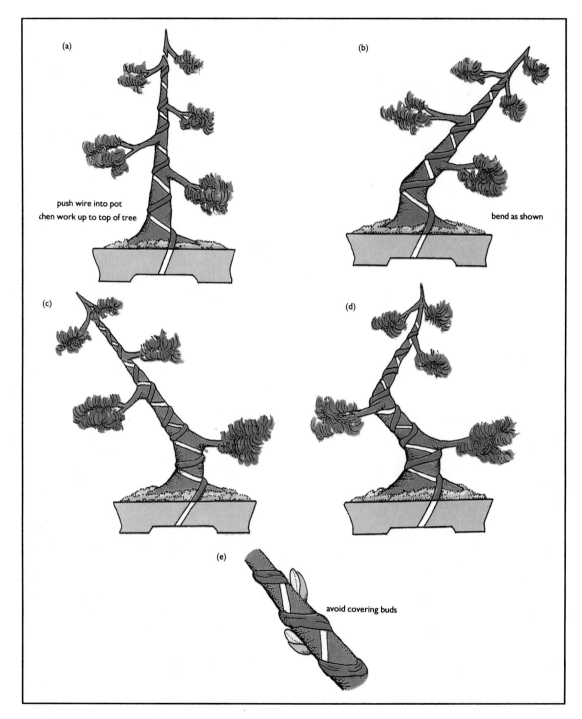

(a)

push wire into pot
then work up to top of tree

(b)

bend as shown

(c)

(d)

(e)

avoid covering buds

Fig 49   Shaping the main trunk with wire. Never allow the wire to cut into the trunk.

wiring two branches
at the same time

wiring one branch only

Fig 50   When wiring, a good anchoring point is very important.

single branches, using the centre or main trunk as an anchoring point. Select two branches close to each other, as shown in Fig 50.

Step two   Cut a piece of wire long enough to wire both branches, then (as shown in Fig 50) start from the middle of the wire and wire branch 'a', then do the same to branch 'b'. The most important thing to remember when wiring double or single branches is to anchor the middle of the wire first.

Remember, this is the basic technique of wiring, designed not to confuse. As you grow in experience, you may slightly change your wiring methods. Therefore, as a general rule, place the wire on the previous season's wood (remember, do not wire young, sappy growth) at the beginning of a growing season.

Year Two

Root Pruning

Indoor bonsai is not governed by the same rules as the outdoor bonsai, basically because of the warmer conditions and the frost-free growing environment. Therefore, with the exception of the flowering period, root pruning and re-potting can take place at almost any time of the year, although it is far better to keep to a root pruning programme.

The time of year I choose is March to April and September to October, favouring March to April as the best time of the year. I have chosen this time of year because the seed or cutting sown or taken in the previous spring is now one year old. This is also the time of year when all the other bonsai, such as hardy bonsai if you have them, need root pruning and re-potting. Therefore you can collate all the work on root systems to one time of the year. It is a good idea to keep a yearly record not only of root pruning, but also of feeding and spraying. This will ensure you do not root prune twice or over-feed.

Step one   First remove the tree from its pot. Work from the sides down to the bottom of the root system, loosening one-third of the root system as in Fig 51 (a).

Step two   Now cut the loosened one-third of roots away from the main root system, as in Figs 51 (b) and 51 (c). At the same time check for signs of pest and disease before re-potting.

Re-potting

Step one   First place a piece of mesh over the drainage hole or holes, then cover this with 6mm washed gravel (Fig 51 (d)).

Step two   Place the tree into the pot, and with a chopstick work fresh compost into the root system, allowing for a small space between the compost level and the top of the pot. This area will allow for watering and stop the compost from being washed away. (*See* Figs 51 (e) to (g).)

Step three   Cover the top of the compost area with 4mm washed gravel, to help keep the compost moist and control weeds (Fig 51 (h)).

47

Fig 51 Root pruning and re-potting. (a) Remove the tree from the pot and, working from the sides down to the bottom, loosen one-third of the root system.

Fig 51 (b) With root pruning shears, remove the bottom third of the root system, including the tap root.

Fig 51 (c) Note the difference between the woody and fine roots.

Fig 51 (d) Cover drainage holes with mesh and gravel. Then cover the gravel with a thin layer of soil.

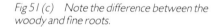

Fig 51 (e)   Place the tree in position (slightly off-centre) and cover roots with fresh soil.

Fig 51 (f)   Work soil between and around the root system with a chopstick.

Fig 51 (g)   Leave a small space between the surface of the compost and the top of the pot to avoid washing away compost when watering.

Fig 51 (h)   Cover the surface of the compost with 4mm gravel. This will help to control weeds and keep the compost surface moist during warm periods.

CHAPTER 5

The Six Basic Shapes

Forming the shape of a bonsai can be a very individual subject and therefore it is very difficult for me to convey my ideas to you. However, there is a basic set of principles relating to each shape and these principles should be made clear before attempting to create your own individual shape.

You must first find an area of angles to work to and desired boundaries to keep within. By this I mean an angle such as 45 or 90 degrees and a boundary of height, width and depth. To do this you must first draw a plan which will enable you to put foresight into the style and shape of your bonsai.

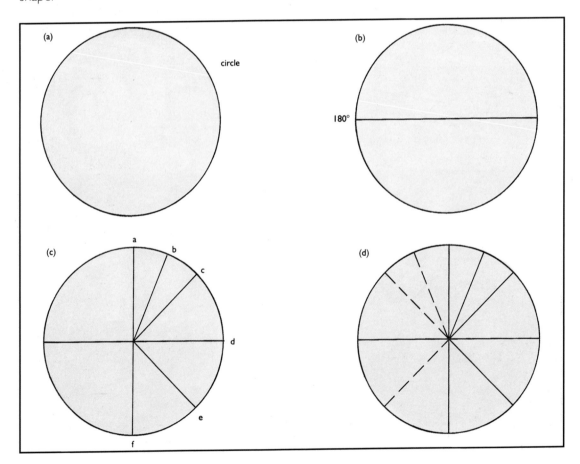

Fig 52   The initial steps in drawing a plan.

ANGLES

First start your plan by drawing a circle as shown in Fig 52 (a). This is your boundary line and will be explained in more detail later. Divide the circle horizontally in half (180 degrees) as in Fig 52 (b).

Divide the top right hand of the circle and mark the sections a, b, c, d, e and f as shown in Fig 52 (c), with 'a' being at 90 degrees.

With a dotted line, draw the same angles on the left-hand side to produce a mirror-image (Fig 52 (d)). This second line will give you the option of shaping the tree to the right or to the left. Provided you always work from a base line, more lined angles for the side (lateral) branches will be added at a later stage once you have become accustomed to using a plan.

Finish off the plan by writing a list below the circle, placing each style next to a letter:

(a)	Formal Upright	(b)	Informal Upright
(c)	Slanting	(d)	Windswept
(e)	Cascade	(f)	Weeping

BOUNDARY

The second part of the plan is to form a boundary of height, width and depth and to do this you will need to draw a second circle the same as the first. The first circle is the one with your angles and letters marked on it and will be called the first dimension circle from now on. It will be used vertically to show the boundary from the bottom to the top plus the sides (height and width) and angles of the trunk and branches of the tree.

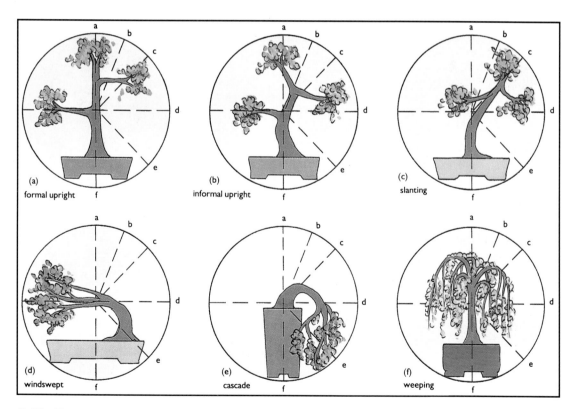

Fig 53   The six basic shapes, as shown in the first dimensional (front) view.

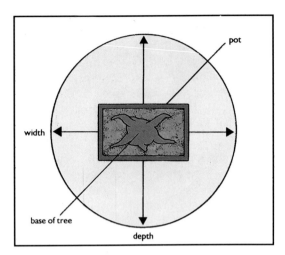

Fig 54   The second dimensional plan, or bird's-eye view, looking down from the top of the tree.

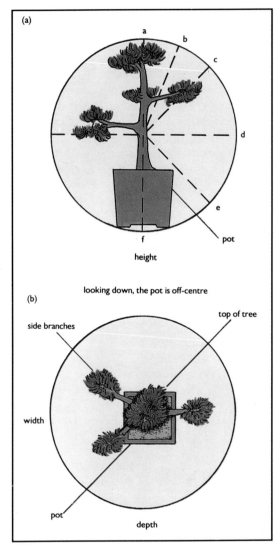

Fig 55   The formal upright. (a) First dimensional plan, showing the branch angles. (b) Second dimensional plan, showing the boundary line.

The second circle, or 'second dimension' circle as it is termed from now on, is the circle which will be used horizontally, to show the boundary from the front to the back and sides (depth and width) and also includes the position for the base of the tree. The rim of the circle, or the 'boundary line', is the main factor in the second dimension circle. The angles are used to show the spacing of the branches from a bird's eye view, as in Fig 54.

At a later stage you may wish to add the angles and boundary line of the first dimension to the second dimension, offering you a back-up system for checking the angles and boundary lines, and at the same time this would give you a third dimension plan. However, I feel that you should initially keep to the first two circles.

By using the two factors of angle and boundary, practise drawing a plan of the style and outline shape of your bonsai as shown in the example (Figs 55 (a) and (b)).

FORMAL UPRIGHT

Although you are growing an indoor bonsai, which means that it will continue to make new growth throughout the year, it would be far better to concentrate on shape and style during the spring and summer months. This is because, due to the lack of light and fluctuations in temperature through heating systems being turned on and off, you may find that the tree's growth will slow down during the winter period.

Fig 56   The beginnings of a formal upright.

However, once your tree has developed large, woody branches it would be advisable to remove any unwanted large branches during the winter period, when the sap flow is not as active as it is during the summer months. In the case of an emergency, such as a broken branch which may cause a disease problem if left unattended, the branch should be pruned whatever time of year it is.

Step one   Whether your seedling comes from seed, cuttings, or is purchased from a nursery, it will make no difference providing the seedling has a straight trunk. If you have not read through the previous chapter on pinching and pruning cuts, do so before going any further. Once you have selected your seedling and have familiarised yourself with pruning techniques, start by drawing a plan showing the height and width of your tree.

Once you have drawn your circle showing these boundaries, pencil in the main trunk at a 90 degree angle as shown in Fig 55 (a). You may, if you

wish, draw in the pot, but some people prefer to use a training pot which in many cases may change every year. In this case draw in the root ball or a line showing where the base of the trunk starts from soil level. Now mark the point, indicating where the lowest branch will start. All buds or growth below this point will be removed (*see* Fig 57).

Now draw in the side branches at 180 degrees. This is your first dimensional plan, indicating the height, width and angle of the trunk and side branches.

Draw a second dimensional plan, or 'bird's eye view', showing the width (front and back as well as sides) and position of the tree in its pot. Again, angles can be applied to this plan which would show the front, side and back growth. This time, as stated before, you are looking down from the top of the tree, a view and angle most people will not see, although an important one from a growing point of view. With the exception of the windswept style (*see* page 58), the second dimensional plan will only be used to show the position of the trunk's base (the bottom of the trunk) when re-potted. When the tree is placed in a bonsai pot, positioning of the trunk is an important factor. Positioning is of less importance when using a training pot, which some people prefer to use through the first stages. This may take five years or more. (Note that most trees are placed slightly off-centre.)

Step two   Now you have your plan, choose the side buds on the main trunk closest to the point indicated on your first dimensional plan (*see* Fig 55 (a)). Keep the chosen bud and remove the rest, as in Fig 57. Allow these side branches to develop during the first year to the width as shown in the boundary line of your first dimensional plan. Once they have reached the boundary line, stop them by pinching out the growing tips which in turn will activate the buds lower down the branch to push out sub-lateral branches.

Using the second dimensional plan, allow the sub-lateral branches to reach their desired

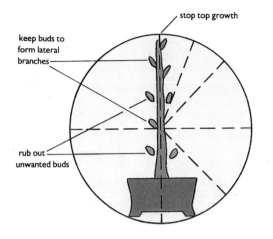

Fig 57   *After choosing the buds you wish to keep, rub out the unwanted ones.*

points either to the boundary line or to a point inside the boundary line.

Step three   Continue to prune and shape your bonsai until you have reached the desired shape. This may take between five and seven years for a basic shape. When a basic shape has

been achieved, only the control of new growth should be continued.

Aftercare   If the tree should start to look unwell during any of the shaping and styling stages, stop the training until the tree has recovered. It is very important that a feeding, watering, and spraying for pest and disease programme is followed throughout the year.

INFORMAL UPRIGHT

Except for the shape of the trunk, the informal upright is the same as the formal upright when it comes to choosing the height, width, depth and buds to produce the side branches, but the trunk is allowed to bend and twist, and be placed into a more creative style. To form the shape of the trunk you may, if you wish, prune back to a bud which is facing the direction in which you would like your trunk to grow (*see* Shaping to a Bud,

Fig 58   *Pomegranate before pruning.*

Fig 59   *The same tree as in Fig 58, after pruning.*

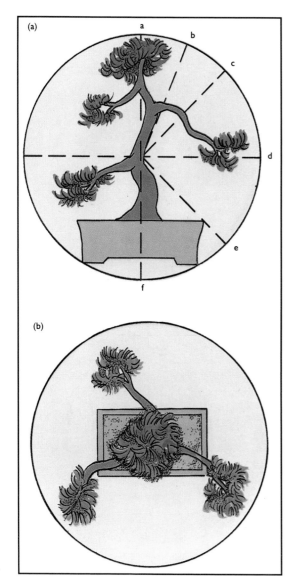

(a)

a

b

c

d

e

f

(b)

*Fig 60   The informal upright. (a) First
dimensional plan. (b) Second dimensional plan*

bends in the trunk,
and spaced branches

branches bent in the
shape of a dragon's back

*Fig 61   Contorted shapes add to the artistic feel
of an informal upright.*

page 44). This is inclined to give a Z–shape if used to shape the complete length of the trunk, so wiring or clamping would be more suitable for this style.

Step one   When you have drawn your first and second dimensional plans, mark in the line as shown at the beginning of this chapter. After you have finished marking all the lines (a), (b), (c) and so on, pencil in two more horizontal lines as shown in Fig 60. These three horizontal lines will now be employed to show where the bends in the main trunk will be formed. Pencil in the trunk as shown in Fig 60. You may also pencil in where the wire will be positioned.

Step two   The branches can be displayed on your plan, remembering to space them alternately as in Fig 60. The side branches should also be trained on an angle similar to the cascade line (d) as shown at the beginning of this chapter and also with a slight bend like the dragon's back in Fig 61.

Step three   By using the second dimensional plan, mark in the position of the base of the tree, the width and depth, then pencil in the trunk showing it as a spiral almost like a spring, as in Fig 61. At the same time pencil on to the plan the side branches and sub-lateral branches (Fig 60).

Step four   Now you are ready to put your plan into action. First find or propagate a seedling slightly taller than is shown on your plan. This will allow for the tree dropping in height due to the spiral effect. Root prune the tree as normal (*see* Root Pruning, pages 47 to 49). The age of seedling you are looking for is between one and two years old. At this stage the trunk should still be pliable, allowing you to bend and twist it to the desired shape. Older trees may need either a thicker grade wire or a clamp.

The most important point to remember when wiring is to anchor the wire. Push the wire firmly into and down to the bottom of the pot. Once you are happy that the wire is anchored, start positioning it up the trunk, remembering not to cover the growing point for the side branches.

Step five Now bend the trunk at the point you have chosen on your plan, at the same time forming the tree into a spiral shape. Pinch out the growing points if they extend above the boundary line of the first dimensional plan. The chosen side branches can be wired using the two-branch system outlined on page 45. Again, stop the growth from going beyond the boundary line. Continue to shape by stopping, rubbing out new growth and adding any further wiring that may be called for. Once the tree has reached its desired shape, pruning back of new growth to keep the tree in check is the only form of training needed.

Aftercare Remove the wire at the end of one growing season, or sooner if it is damaging the bark in any way. Follow a watering, feeding and spraying programme for pest and diseases throughout the year.

ROUND HEAD (BROOM STYLE)

As with all the other shapes and styles in this chapter, pruning should be carried out during the spring and summer months, which in this country is the chief growing season. The exception is large woody branches, which cause less of a problem if removed during the winter months.

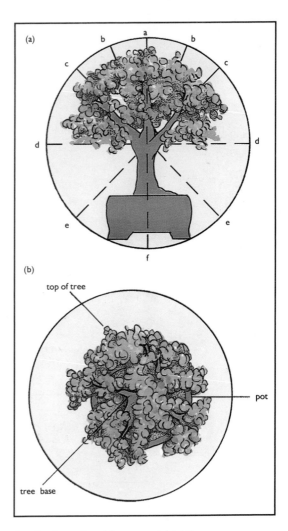

Fig 62 Round head (broom style). (a) First dimensional plan. (b) Second dimensional plan.

Most of the indoor bonsai trees will lend themselves to a round head shape, but for this example we will use a myrthus, one of the reasons being that the head of the tree will need regular attention during the growing season by pinching back the growing tips (*see* Pinching and Pruning, page 44). When doing this you will appreciate the aroma given off by the scented foliage. Before going any further I would suggest you read through temperatures and likes and dislikes of the tree, which can be found on page 79.

Fig 63   Pinching out a growing tip. (a) Unpruned myrtle (seven years old).

Fig 63 (b)   Pinching back new growth.

Fig 63 (c)   The myrtle after pruning.

Step one   Start by propagating from seed or cuttings, or purchasing a small myrthus seedling. For those who are growing from seed or cuttings, do not prune the roots during the first year, but for those who have purchased a seedling, try as far as possible to buy your seedling at the beginning of the year (March to April). The seedling should be at least one year old to root prune straight away. If younger than one year, wait until the following March before touching the root system, but continue to shape and style the top of the tree. *See* Root Pruning, pages 47 to 49.

Step two   Start by using the first and second dimensional plans and show the angle, and boundary of the height, width and depth of the tree you wish to create. The height for the first-time grower should be kept between 15–30cm (6–12in). Again by using the plan, choose the trunk's angle which may be straight (90 degrees) or have a slight slant (between 90 and 45

degrees), as in Fig 62, and pencil the line of the trunk on to your plan.

Step three The next stage is to form a neck or point from which the branches will start to form the head. This is done by removing all the buds up to a chosen point as shown in Fig 63.

Three or four buds above this point should be chosen very carefully and pencilled in on your first dimensional plan to form the main branch system which will produce sub-lateral branches and eventually, between three to five years later, produce a bonsai with a rounded head.

Step four Once you have decided on the height, width, depth, buds to grow and buds to take out, pinch out or prune back to the growing tips and appointed areas as pencilled in on your plans. If you have not read through the section on pinching out the top growth, do so before attempting to go any further.

Pinching, small branch pruning, most types of wiring and leaf pruning should be carried out during the growing months, which in most cases is between March and October. Large branch pruning should be carried out between the months of January and the end of February, unless a branch should break during the summer months, which may cause die-back if left unattended.

Aftercare All shaping and styling should stop if the tree starts to look unwell. Only continue when the tree is showing strong healthy growth. Follow a feeding, watering, spraying for pest and disease programme throughout the year.

WINDSWEPT

Trees that are found in exposed areas such as cliff tops, downs and large, open spaces tend to have most of their branches bending away from the exposed side of the tree, as shown in Fig 64. Therefore, along with your two plans you will also need to add the appearance of a roughness

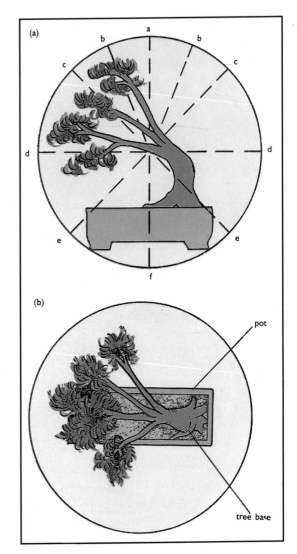

Fig 64   Windswept. (a) First dimensional plan.
(b) Second dimensional plan.

which is found in trees growing in exposed areas. This may be straightforward when planting over rock (*see* Chapter 8), because the hardness of the rock helps to create the illusion of a wild and barren area, but without rock it will not be so easy. A shallow dish will help to create such an illusion, like the oval-shaped dish in Fig 96. Here the tree is placed towards one end on a slant, with its branches allowed to extend almost to the other end of the dish. For those who choose to use a training pot for the first five years, a seed tray with extra drainage holes will serve the purpose.

Step one   Put pen to paper and make two plans on how the tree will look, as outlined at the beginning of this chapter. For those who purchase their seedlings, try as far as possible to find a seedling with a trunk that is slanted, but for those of you who grow from seed or cuttings, wait until the bark becomes woody then wire the trunk and bend it to the desired angle.

The plans should also show height, width, depth and the buds which need to be trained and those which need to be removed. In most of the other planned styles in this chapter I have mentioned the problem of deciding where the tree should be placed in its pot, but with the windswept style it is very important that the position is shown at the start, and if a training pot is used then the correct shape of container should be found.

Once you have your seedling and container, root prune if it is the right time of the year and re-pot as outlined on pages 47 to 49. Remember to keep the trunk to the angle shown on your first dimensional plan.

Step two   Allow the side branches to reach the point you have chosen inside your boundary line. In most cases I suggest that you train to buds and avoid too much wiring, but in the case of the windswept style, the branches should look as if they have been bent and twisted by wind turbulence as shown in Fig 64 (a). The branches will at some stage need wiring and twisting to give this illusion.

Once you have created your basic shape, which may take as long as five years, continue to remove unwanted new growth only.

Aftercare   A feeding, watering and pest and disease programme should be followed throughout the year.

Fig 65   Tall and short cascade pots with measuring chart.

CASCADE

This style is often confused with the weeping style. Fig 66 (c) and (d) show the difference. Notice how the cascade, although still a form of weeping, tends to have a greater angle on its branches; almost an inverted V–shape, but with the weeping style, it takes on an inverted U–shape.

Step one   As with all the other styles, start first by drawing a plan to show all the boundaries, but before you start, look at the first dimensional plan shown in Fig 66 (a). In the plan you will see that the pot height will need to be positioned as shown and in this example the pot takes up the bottom section of the circle. We use such a tall pot like the one shown in Fig 65 to give the branches plenty of room to cascade down to the bottom of the pot.

Because the cascade style lends itself to such a tall pot you will have to change the root pruning procedure slightly. You will need a longer root system than you would when growing other styles such as a formal upright. The procedure is

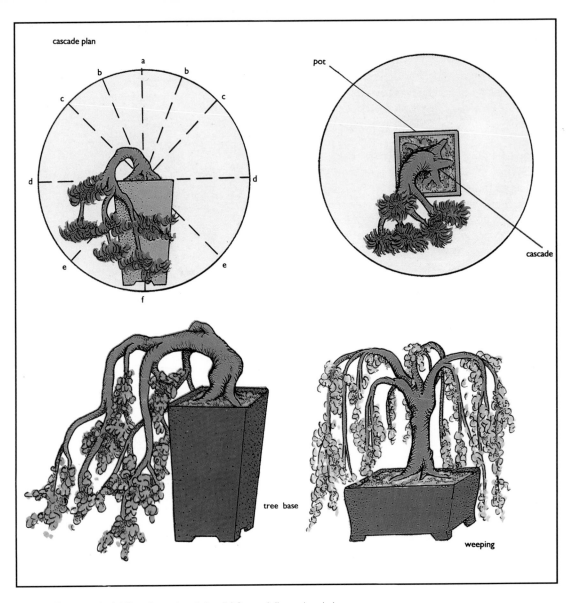

Fig 66   The cascade. (a) First dimensional plan. (b) Second dimensional plan.
(c) and (d) Showing the differences between the two shapes.

basically the same as for normal root pruning, but during the first two years or until the root system reaches the bottom of the pot, loosen one-third of the root system as normal, but do not cut the complete section. Instead, tease the large, woody roots away from the fine roots and take out these large woody roots only. Once the root system has reached its desired length, follow the normal root pruning procedure (*see* Root Pruning).

Step two   Now decide upon, and pencil in on your plan, the angle of the trunk and the side from which the branches will form. Remember that the trunk will bend at the appointed area and start to cascade down, but the first few centimetres from the base of the trunk may be at the angle of a formal upright, informal upright, or slanting. This is a decision for you to take (*see* Fig 68). All the buds below the point where the

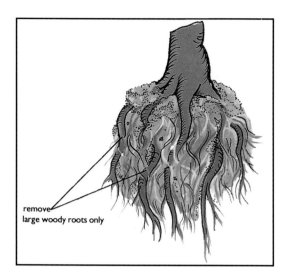

remove
large woody roots only

Fig 67   When growing a cascade shape, only the
large, thick, woody roots should be removed.
The fibrous root system should be encouraged to
extend the full length of the pot.

trunk bends should be marked on your plan for
taking out. In other words, the trunk from the
base to the bend will be free from any growth, as
in Fig 68.

Once you have specified the point where the
trunk will bend, pencil in the trunk following the
angle (d) as shown in the plan on page 60 for the
cascade shape (Fig 66). When you have finished
marking the trunk, define which buds should be
left to grow and which ones are to be taken out.
Those buds left to grow are the starting point for
the main and sub-lateral branches.

When you have finished your plan and found
the right seedling, pot or training container, start
by taking out those large woody roots (if it is the
correct time of year) then re-pot and start
shaping the first stage of the trunk, followed by
the second stage. Allow the buds left on the
second stage of the trunk to grow until they
reach the desired point and then stop their
growing tips, to produce sub-lateral branches.

Aftercare   Follow a watering, feeding and pest
and disease spraying programme throughout
the year.

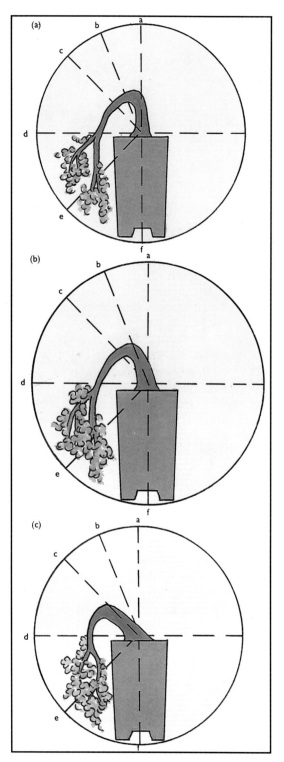

Fig 68   Three ways in which the main angle of
the trunk may be grown.

61

CHAPTER 6

An A–Z of Indoor Trees

There are many forms of trees and shrubs from the warmer regions of the world that will grow as an indoor bonsai. In fact it would take two or three books to list them all. I have therefore listed those which I have personally tried and tested. Although some will never form into a true tree shape such as the forms found growing in our English countryside, they will make interesting artistic and abstract shapes full of charm and grace by using other materials such as driftwood and colourful decorative pots.

In the list that follows I have tried to simplify the names of the plants used by using the common name first, and the botanical second. However, do try to learn some of the botanical names if possible.

Note – Placement The obvious position for most indoor bonsai is close to the window. This is fine between the late spring and early autumn, but during the winter time the bonsai should be moved away from the window during the night to avoid frost damage. Even with central heating and double glazing, the temperature between the window and curtain may drop very low. Also note that bonsai, or indeed any indoor plant, should not be positioned on top of a television.

ACACIA (*Acacia karoo*)

This yellow-flowering deciduous tree with its fern-like leaves and white thorns will make an excellent indoor bonsai. Coming from South Africa it will tolerate the warmer conditions of indoor cultivation.

Position Plenty of light and good ventilation.
Temperature Winter never below 4°C (39°F).
Watering Every day during the summer, every two to three days during the winter.
Propagation Seed or cuttings.
Seed Sow seeds in April in compost Code 1, at a temperature of 16°C (61°F).
Cuttings Sow a young, semi-ripe cutting with a heel between the months of April and May, in a compost Code 2 at a temperature between 16–18°C (61–64°F).
Compost Code 4.
Root prune Every year up to five years old, then every two years.
Pest Mealybug, caterpillars, red spider mite.
Disease Wilt, die-back.

Azalea *see* Rhododendron.

BANANA (*Musa taiwan*)

Deciduous dwarf banana tree from China. To produce the fruit for showing you would need to grow a large specimen bonsai; therefore this is not a tree for the beginner. A small form from the Canary Islands is *Musa cavendisbii/Musa acuminata* or 'Dwarf Cavendish'.

Position Light shade from May to August. Winter full light.
Temperature Never allow the temperature to drop below 10°C (50°F) during the winter. Summer, keep the temperature below 21°C (70°F).
Watering Every day during the summer, every two to three days during the winter.

Propagation   Sow seed in April in a compost Code 1, with a temperature of 21°C (70°F).
Compost   Code 4.
Root prune   Every two to three years. Not a tree for the beginner, troublesome.
Pest   Red spider mite.
Disease   Mildew; allow plenty of ventilation.

BAOBAB (*Adansonia digitata*)

The baobab is a very large, deciduous tree found in parts of Africa and is famous for its trunk which is shaped like a bottle. It is said that this tree can live to a great age. This is not a bonsai for the beginner.

Position   Plenty of light, good ventilation.
Temperature   Between 16–18°C (61–64°F).
Watering   Every day during the summer, every two to three days during the winter.
Propagation   Seed sown in April in a compost Code 1, with a temperature of 21°C (70°F).
Compost   Code 4.
Root prune   Every year up to five years, then every two to three years.
Pest   Red spider mite.
Disease   Wilt, mildew. Allow air to flow freely around the bonsai.

BARBADOS CHERRY (*Malpighia glabra/Malpighia coccigera*)

Interesting evergreen tree from the West Indies. Can be trained into a delightful bonsai which produces pink flowers.

Position   Plenty of light but not direct sunlight.
Temperature   Should not drop below 18°C (64°F) and never be above 24°C (75°F).
Watering   Every day during the summer, every two to three days during the winter.
Propagation   Seed and cuttings.
Seed   April in a compost Code 1, with a temperature of 21°C (70°F).

Cuttings   April, softwood cuttings in compost Code 2, bottom heat 21–25°C (70–77°F).
Compost   Code 4.
Pest   Aphids, red spider mite.
Disease   Mainly free, but prune to allow light and air into the centre of the tree.

BEEFWOOD TREE (*Casuarina equisetifolia*)

An evergreen tree from Malaya with tufted needles. Can make an unusual indoor bonsai and is fairly easy to grow. Another small Casuarina with the common name of 'Dwarf Sheoke', is *Casuarina nana* which is a small Australian shrub, again quite easy to grow and a good tree for the beginner.

Position   Plenty of light, but not direct sunlight.
Temperature   16–18°C (61–64°F).
Watering   Every day during the summer, every two to three days during the winter.
Propagation   Seed sown in compost Code 1, with a temperature of 16°C (61°F).
Compost   Code 4.
Root prune   Every year up to five years, then every two years.
Pest   Aphids, red spider mite.
Disease   Mainly free.

BLUE GUM (*Eucalyptus globulus*)

This tender evergreen tree from Tasmania will make attractive, colourful indoor bonsai and is used by some gardens as a bedding plant during the summer months. It is therefore often available from local nurseries. Its blue-white, smooth bark adds to the attraction of this interesting bonsai with white flowers and large black fruits.

Position   Plenty of light and full sun, place outside on warm days during the summer.
Temperature   Cold room with a temperature about 16°C (61°F).

Fig 69 *Bottle tree with an unusual-shaped trunk.*

Watering Every day during the summer, every two to three days during the winter.
Propagation Seed sown in February to March in compost Code 1, with a temperature of 13–16°C (55–61°F). Cover seed tray with a propagator top.
Compost Code 4, keep compost moist during the summer months.
Root prune Carefully root prune every two to four years then every three. Roots can be temperamental when pruned.
Pest Mainly free.
Disease Mainly free.

For other Eucalyptus, *see* Cider Gum and Lemon.

BOTTLE TREE
(*Brachychiton ruspestris*)

The bottle tree, which comes from north-east Australia, has a very thick and unusual shaped trunk and because it comes from a warm country will tolerate very dry conditions. This makes it an excellent indoor bonsai for the beginner.

Position Plenty of light, will even tolerate direct sunlight.
Temperature Between 10–24°C (50–75°F).
Watering Check compost every three days during the summer, but as a general rule water once a week. Winter – water once a fortnight, but continue to test the compost, never letting it completely dry out.
Compost Code 3.
Propagation Mature trees can be purchased from your bonsai centre at a fairly low cost.
Root prune Every three years.
Pest Red spider mite.
Disease Mainly free.

CARMONA
(*Carmona microphylla*)

Evergreen shrub with a white flower and fol- lowed by a berry, reddish in colour. Very tree- like without too much training.

Position   Plenty of light, but not direct sunlight.
Temperature   Between 15–24°C (59–75°F).
Watering   Every day during the summer, every two to three days during the winter.
Compost   Code 4.
Propagation   Seed and cuttings.
Seed   Sow seeds in compost Code 1, at a temperature between 16–18°C (61–64°F).
Cuttings   Soft wood or semi-ripe in compost Code 2, at a temperature of 18°C (64°F).
Root prune   Every year up to five, then every two years.
Pest   Aphids, red spider mite.
Disease   Die-back, wilt.

CAROB (*Ceratonia siliqua*)

The common name for this evergreen tree is 'St John's Bread'. Very easy to grow, making it an ideal indoor bonsai for the beginner.

Position   Plenty of light.
Temperature   Between 16–18°C (61–64°F).
Watering   Every day during the summer, every two to three days during the winter.
Propagation   Seed, sown in compost Code 1, with a temperature of 16°C (61°F).
Compost   Code 4.
Root prune   Every year up to five years, then every two years.
Pest   Mainly free.
Disease   Mainly free.

CHINESE SACRED BAMBOO
(*Nandina domestica*)

The sacred bamboo is a small shrub from China, and given time it will form into a cold room, flowering bonsai. The flowers are white and show themselves during the month of July. This is followed by a white fruit in August. This is really a semi-indoor bonsai and therefore will need a rest period through the winter. Its advantage, however, is the autumn colour just before the bonsai drops some of its old foliage.

Position   Cool room, but frost-free. Plenty of light during the winter and summer and good ventilation.
Temperature   Winter temperature 10°C (50°F), but will tolerate lower temperatures. Summer temperature between 16–18°C (61–64°F).
Watering   Every day during the summer, twice a week during the winter.
Propagation   Seed and cuttings.
Seed   Seeds are sown in seed trays and placed outside to over-winter in compost Code 1, without bottom heat.
Cuttings   Treat them the same as a hardwood cutting, but place in a pot or tray and then in a cold frame or glasshouse.
Compost   Code 4.
Root prune   Every year up to five then every two years.
Pest   Mainly free.
Disease   Mainly trouble-free, but prune to allow light and air into the centre of the tree.

CHINESE WATER ELM
(*Ulmus parvifolia*)

Semi-evergreen cold room indoor bonsai which produces a small, thick trunk in a short space of time and therefore will look more tree-like than most other indoor bonsai.

Position   Place in a cool position with plenty of

Fig 70 *Sacred bamboo with driftwood.*

Fig 71   Chinese water elm, displayed with decorative objects.

Fig 72   Chinese water elm, an excellent cold room bonsai.

light. Place outside from mid-May to September, avoid frost.

Temperature   Summer temperature between 10–22°C (50–72°F), winter temperature should not fall below 6°C (43°F).

Watering   Every day during the summer months, every two to three days during the winter.

Propagation   Seed or cuttings, softwood or semi-ripe.

Compost   Code 4.

Root prune   Every year up to five then every two to three years, depending on the rate of growth.

Pest   Mainly free.

Disease   Mainly free.

CHRISTMAS TORCH
(*Metrosideros tomentosa*)

Given time this evergreen tree from New Zealand will make an excellent bonsai, producing flowers which resemble candles. Because of this, the tree is also called the Christmas Tree.

Position Plenty of light, but not direct sunlight.
Temperature Between 16–18°C (61–64°F).
Watering Every day during the summer, every two to three days during the winter.
Propagation Seed sown in compost Code 4, at a temperature of 18°C (64°F).
Compost Code 4.
Root prune Every year up to five then every two years.
Pest Mainly free.
Disease Mainly free.

CIDER GUM (*Eucalyptus gunnii*)

Found in southern areas of Australia and also grown in parts of England. This evergreen Eucalyptus would be classed as a cold room bonsai and placed outside during the summer months. It has a very attractive bark which is smooth and grey, and has white, fluffy flowers which form in clusters of three, followed by white flat-ended capsules.

Position Plenty of light, outside on warm days.
Temperature Cold room, with a temperature of 16°C (61°F).
Watering Every day during the summer, every two to three days during the winter.
Propagation Seed sown between February and March in compost Code 1, with a temperature of 13–16°C (55–61°F), cover seed tray with propagator lid or a piece of glass.
Compost Code 4, keep moist during the summer months.
Root prune Prune every two years up to four then every three years. Care should be taken, roots are prone to rotting.

Fig 73 A young eucalyptus used as a cold room bonsai.

Pest   Mainly free.
Disease   Mainly free.

For other Eucalyptus *see* Blue Gum and Lemon.

CITRON (*Citrus medica*)

This small-growing tree from the Far East can make an excellent semi-cold room indoor bonsai. The flowers, which are pinkish-white and fragrant, tend to be too large for the tree. The fruits would be too heavy for the small, fine branches of a bonsai, and therefore it would be better to remove the flowers once they have gone over or just before they set seed.

Position   Plenty of light.
Temperature   Between 18–21°C (64–70°F); never allow winter temperatures to fall below 13°C (55°F).
Watering   Every day during the summer, every two to three days during the winter.
Propagation   Seed or cuttings.
Seed   Sow seeds in compost Code 1, at a temperature of 16°C (61°F).
Cuttings   Semi-ripe, with bottom heat at a temperature of 18°C (64°F).
Compost   Code 4.
Root prune   Every two years up to six then every three years.
Pest   Red spider mite.
Disease   Mainly free.

For other Citrus *see* Grapefruit, Lemon, Orange, Seville Orange, Sweet Orange and Tangerine.

CORAL TREE (*Erythrina indica*)

This deciduous tree from India can be trained into a fascinating flowering indoor bonsai. Two common names given to this tree are 'Crab Claw' and 'Tiger's Claw'. The tree owes its common names to the shape of the flowers

Fig 74   A young coral tree.

which are in the shape of a claw. The flowers are crimson and followed by very attractive pods.

Position   Light shade through the summer months.
Temperature   Never allow the winter temperature to drop below 7°C (45°F) Summer – place in a cool room with a temperature of 16°C (61°F).
Watering   Every day during the summer, every two to three days during the winter.
Propagation   Seed or cuttings.
Seed   Sow in compost Code 1, at a temperature of 16°C (61°F).
Cuttings   Taken with a heel.
Root prune   Every year up to five then every two or three years depending on the rate of growth.
Pest   Red spider mite.
Disease   Mainly free.

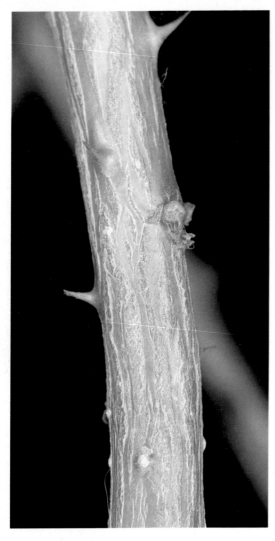

Fig 75   The coral tree in close-up – note the attractive trunk with its deadly thorns.

DATE PALM (*Phoenix roebelenii*)

This evergreen palm from Asia will make an excellent indoor bonsai especially when grown in volcanic rock.

Position   Light shade and good ventilation. Keep the compost between dry and moist during the winter months.

Watering   The palm will need plenty of water during the summer months, plus misting with a hand spray. For those grown in the soft forms of volcanic or tufa rock, you may find you need to water twice a day during the summer. Winter, water every two to three days and mist to help control red spider mite.

Temperature   Never allow the temperature to drop below 13°C (55°F) during the winter months. Summer temperature should be 18°C (64°F).

Propagation   Seed and suckers.

Seed   Sow between February and March in a compost Code 1, with a temperature between 18–21°C (64–70°F).

Suckers   Suckers can be transplanted during the month of May into individual training pots with compost Code 3 and kept at a temperature between 18–21°C (64–70°F). Removing suckers is also a form of pruning, therefore no other pruning is required.

Compost   Code 3 or volcanic rock and tufa.

Root pruning   Every two years for pot grown, no root pruning when grown in rock or tufa.

Pest   Mealybugs, red spider mite.

Disease   Mainly free.

Also *see* Parlour Palm.

Fig 76   A normal house plant palm can look attractive when grown in a piece of tufa.

DRAGON TREE
(*Dracaena draco*)

A good, evergreen indoor bonsai from the Canary Islands and an excellent tree for the beginner which has a very attractive root system when exposed in a flat bonsai dish. One of the longer living trees, said to live up to 1,000 years old, such as the well-known dragon tree used as a show piece on one of the Canary Islands.

Position   Plenty of light and good ventilation.
Temperature   Winter temperature of 10°C (50°F), but will tolerate slightly lower temperatures. Summer temperatures 16–18°C (61–64°F).
Watering   Every day during the summer, every two to three days during the winter.
Propagation   Cuttings. Most good garden centres with a houseplant section should be able to supply you with your first seedling or plant. Form this 7.5cm (3in) mature stem cutting, taken in April, and place in a compost Code 2 on a warm bench or in a propagator at a temperature of 21°C (70°F).
Compost   Code 4.
Root prune   Carefully prune the root every two years. Do not over water for the next three weeks, stop feeding for one month.
Pest   Root mealybug, red spider mite.
Disease   Mainly free.

FIG (*Ficus deltoidea/ Ficus diversifolia*)

Small evergreen tree from India. It is commonly known as the 'Mistletoe Fig' or 'Cherry Banyan' and produces yellow-red fruits. A good fruiting bonsai for the beginner.

Position   Plenty of light but not direct sunlight and good ventilation.
Temperature   Winter temperature 10°C (50°F). Summer temperature 16–18°C (61–64°F).
Watering   Every day during the summer, every two to three days during the winter.

Fig 77   A dragon tree makes an unusual but interesting bonsai.

Fig 78   A young fig.

Propagation   Plant should be available from good garden centres with houseplant sections, or from cuttings and air-layering.
Cuttings   Cuttings can be taken between the months of April and June. Take side shoots between 7.5–10cm (3–4in) long and place them in compost Code 2 at 18°C (64°F).
Air-layering   See propagation section on air-layering (page 38).
Compost   Code 4.
Root prune   Every two years. Roots can be temperamental.
Pest   Scale insects.
Disease   Root rot.

GARDENIA
(*Gardenia jasminoides*)

This small shrub-like tree can make an excellent flowering bonsai, but is not a tree for the beginner. The tree will flower from June to August; flowers are white and very scented.

Position   Plenty of light during the winter, part shade in the summer with good ventilation.
Temperature   Winter temperature between 12–16°C (54–61°F). Summer temperature between 16–18°C (61–64°F).
Watering   Every day during the summer. Keep the atmosphere humid during warm, sunny days by using a humidity tray or mist spray gun (do not mist in direct sunlight). In winter, water every two to three days.
Propagation   The first plant can be purchased from a garden centre with a house plant section, and then take cuttings.
Cuttings   Non-flowering side shoots taken with a heel during the months of February to March in a compost Code 2 at a temperature of 18–21°C (64–70°F).
Compost   Code 4.
Root prune   Every two years.
Pest   Aphids, red spider mite, (see Pests and Diseases, page 106).
Disease   Bud drop.

GRAPEFRUIT (*Citrus paradisi*)

The grapefruit can be trained into a semi-cold room indoor bonsai. Flowers are white and fruits are far too large for bonsai; therefore remove flowers before they set seed.

Position   Part shade during the summer months, full light during the winter. Keep the compost moist through the summer.
Temperature   Winter temperature between 7–10°C (45–50°F), summer 18°C (64°F).
Watering   Every day during the summer, every two to three days during the winter.
Propagation   Seed and cuttings.
Seed   Sow seeds in March in compost Code 1 at a temperature of 16°C (61°F).
Cuttings   Take semi-ripe cuttings 7.5–10cm (3–4in) during the months of July and August, in compost Code 2 with a bottom heat temperature of 18°C (64°F).
Compost   Code 4.
Root prune   Grapefruits do not like root pruning, therefore prune every three years in October to November.
Pest   Mealybug.
Disease   Mainly free.

For other Citrus see Citron, Lemon, Orange, Seville Orange, Sweet Orange and Tangerine.

JACQUELINE ELM (*Ulmus x elegantissima* 'Jacqueline Hiller')

Although classed as an indoor bonsai, this small elm is far better suited to a cool, frost-free conservatory with good ventilation. An ideal tree for the beginner who wishes to avoid the problems of maintaining a high temperature.

Position   Light or part shade, cool room with plenty of ventilation.
Temperature   10–18°C (50–64°F) but allow temperature to drop slightly lower to allow for a dormant season; avoid frost.

73

Fig 79   Jacqueline elm showing the beginnings of an interesting shape.

Watering   Every day during the summer, keep soil moist but not too wet during the winter.
Propagation   Seed or cuttings.
Compost   Code 4.
Root prune   Every year up to five, then every two or three years depending on the rate of growth.
Pest   Mainly free.
Disease   Mainly free.

JADE TREE (*Crassula*, many forms)

In past years this has been classed as a house plant rather than a bonsai, although the Japanese have been using it for several years as an indoor bonsai. Another common name is the 'Money Tree' which is very easy to look after and an excellent tree for the beginner. However, the jade can become top heavy if left unpruned.

Position   Good light and plenty of sun.
Temperature   Winter temperature should not fall below 10°C (50°F), although it will tolerate slightly lower temperatures. Summer temperatures between 16–18°C (61–64°F).
Watering   Every one to two days during the summer, every three to four days during the winter.

Fig 80   Jade – a tree which is very easy to propagate.

Propagation Very easy from leaf cuttings. During the spring remove a leaf and allow it to dry for a day or two, then pin to the surface of compost Code 2.
Compost Code 4.
Root prune Every three years. Keep pinching back top growth.
Pest Mealybug.
Disease Mainly free.

JAPANESE PAGODA TREE (*Sophora japonica*)

A small tree from China and Korea which can be trained into a cold room flowering bonsai. It has white, pea-like flowers followed by long pods containing the seed.

Position Plenty of light and sun, good ventilation. Can be kept outside in a south-facing position during a warm summer, but keep it out of strong winds.
Temperature Winter temperature of 10°C (50°F), summer temperature between 16–18°C (61–64°F).
Watering Every day during the summer, every two to three days during the winter.
Propagation Sow seeds during the months of March and April in compost Code 1. In a cold frame or glasshouse, no heat is required.
Compost Code 4.
Root prune Every year up to five, then every two years.
Pest Mainly free.
Disease Mainly free.

JERUSALEM PINE (*Pinus halefecis*)

A form of pine which can be grown indoors, providing cold room condition can be given. Although this pine will make an excellent bonsai, it may be troublesome until you can find a balanced position offering a low temperature without frost and good ventilation.

Fig 81   An indoor pine grown as a cold room bonsai; this tree needs frost-free conditions.

Position Plenty of light in a cool room with good ventilation away from radiators and warm air ducts.
Temperature 10–18°C (50–64°F) throughout the year.
Watering Every day during the summer, every two to three days during the winter.
Propagation Seed or cuttings.
Compost Code 4.
Root prune Every year up to five then every two or three years depending on the rate of growth.
Pest Red spider mite.
Disease Mildew.

75

KOWHAI (*Sophora tetraptera*)

Slow-growing tree from New Zealand, also called New Zealand Laburnum. Good cold room indoor flowering bonsai for the beginner. The flowers are yellow and are followed by long pods containing the seed.

KOWHAI (*Sophora microphylla*)

Again from New Zealand, smaller in height than *Sophora tetraptera*, but with the same coloured flower which shows itself between the months of April and May, followed by long pods containing seed.

Position   Plenty of light and sun, good ventilation. Place outside in a south-facing position during warm summer days out of cold winds.
Temperature   Winter temperature 10°C (50°F), summer between 16–18°C (61–64°F).
Watering   Every day during the summer, every three days during the winter.
Propagation   Sow seeds during the months of March and April in compost Code 1. In a cold frame or glasshouse, no heat is required.
Compost   Code 4.
Root prune   Every year up to five then every two years.
Pest   Mainly free.
Disease   Mainly free.

LEMON (*Citrus limon*)

Small-growing tree from East Asia and less hardy than other Citrus bonsai. It should therefore be grown in a constant warm temperature with plenty of light. The tree has fragrant flowers, followed by the fruit. The fruit would be too large for a small bonsai and can take up to one year to ripen. Therefore, unless you are growing it as a large specimen bonsai, I would suggest you remove the flower heads once they have gone over.

Position   Full light, but not direct sunlight, good ventilation.
Temperature   Winter temperature of 10°C (50°F), summer temperature about 18°C (64°F).
Watering   Every day during the summer, every two to three days during the winter.
Propagation   Seed or cuttings.
Seed   Sow in March with a Code 1 compost at a temperature of 16°C (61°F).
Cuttings   Semi-ripe cuttings taken in the last two weeks of July or the first two weeks of August. Place them in a compost Code 2 with bottom heat at a temperature of 18°C (64°F).
Compost   Code 4.
Root prune   The lemon trees do not like root pruning. Therefore prune every three years between the months of November and December. After pruning do not over water for the next two to four weeks and do not feed for four weeks.
Pest   Mealybug.
Disease   Mainly free.

For other Citrus *see* Citron, Orange, Seville Orange, Sweet Orange.

LEMON (*Eucalyptus citriodora*)

Now you can see why common names can become confusing. This is a form of eucalyptus with leaves that are scented of lemon, adding to the attractive stems and making it a prized bonsai to collect.

Position   Plenty of light, place outside on warm days.
Temperature   Cold room with a temperature of 10°C (50°F).
Watering   Every day during the summer, every two to three days during the winter.
Propagation   Seed sown between February to March in compost Code 1, with a temperature between 13–16°C (55–61°F).
Compost   Code 4, keep moist during the summer months.

Fig 82   Malayan apple, the one in the blue pot showing flowering buds.

Root prune   Every two years up to five, then every three years. Take care when root pruning – roots are prone to rotting.
Pest   Red spider mite, mealy bug.
Disease   Mainly free.

MALAYAN APPLE (*Pitanga*)

This tree makes a very interesting flowering bonsai, with white, fluffy flowers. This is followed later in the season by small fruit which is red to purple in colour and resembles a crab apple fruit as shown in Fig 83.

Position   Full light, but not direct sunlight, good ventilation.
Temperature   Winter temperature should not drop below 10°C (50°F), summer between 16–21°C (61–70°F).
Watering   Every two to three days during the summer, once or twice a week in the winter.

Fig 83   Malayan apple fruit (enlarged).

77

Propagation   Grow from seed or cuttings.
Compost   Code 4.
Root prune   Every year up to five, then every two years.
Pest   Mainly free.
Disease   Mainly free.

MIMOSA (*Acacia dealbata*)

This fast-growing tree from Australia has a silvery fern-like foliage which gives it its common name 'Silver Wattle' or 'Mimosa'. Globular heads of small, bright yellow flowers in clusters appear along its branches making it a colourful bonsai.

Position   Plenty of light with good ventilation.
Temperature   Never below 4°C (39°F) during the winter, otherwise the Acacia will wilt. General temperature between 15–18°C (59–64°F).
Watering   Every day during the summer, every two to three days during the winter.
Propagation   Seed or cuttings.
Seed   Sown in April in a seed compost Code 1, with a temperature of 16°C (61°F).
Cuttings   Between softwood and semi-ripe with a heel, between the months of April and May, in compost Code 2 with bottom heat at a temperature of 16–18°C (61–64°F).
Compost   Code 4.
Root prune   Every year up to five, then every two years.
Pest   Mealybug, tortrix caterpillars if placed outside during the summer.
Disease   Mainly free.

MONKEY PUZZLE (*Araucaria araucana*)

An evergreen tree from Chile which will make an excellent cold room bonsai and a good bonsai for the beginner. There is also the less hardy form called the 'Norfolk Island Pine' (*Araucaria heterophylla*), but this does not form such a good shape as the *Araucaria araucana*.

Fig 84   A young monkey puzzle, a strange but interesting bonsai.

Position   Plenty of light and good ventilation, in a frost-free room.
Temperature   Winter temperature between 5–10°C (41–50°F), summer temperature between 16–18°C (61–64°F).
Watering   Every day during the summer, every two to three days during the winter.
Propagation   Seed sown in March in compost Code 1, at a temperature of 13°C (55°F).
Compost   Code 4.
Root prune   Every year up to five then every two years.
Pest   Mainly free.
Disease   Mainly free.

Fig 85   Two young myrtles with scented foliage.

MYRTLE (*Myrthus communis*)

This evergreen tree from Greece can make a good cold room flowering bonsai with aromatic leaves. The shrub starts flowering in June and can last until August. The flowers are white and are followed by purple to black fruits.

Position   Plenty of light and part sun, good ventilation. Keep compost moist during the summer months.

Temperature   Winter temperature between 5–10°C (41–50°F), summer temperature between 16–18°C (61–64°F).

Watering   Every day during the summer, every two or three days during the winter.

Propagation   Purchase your first plant from the houseplant section of a good garden centre or bonsai nursery and use it as a stock plant to take cuttings.

Cuttings   Take non-flowering side shoots between 5–7.5cm (3–4in) in length, with a heel. Use compost Code 2 and a bottom heat temperature of 16°C (61°F).

Compost   Code 4.

Root prune   Every year up to five years then every two years.

Pest   Mainly free.

Disease   Mainly free.

Fig 86   A young olive suitable for a cold room bonsai.

OLIVE TREE (*Olea*)

The olive tree will make a very suitable evergreen indoor cold room bonsai, but will take several years before it starts to fruit.

Position   Plenty of light, but not direct sunlight.
Temperature   During the winter period temperatures should remain at 10°C (50°F), but the bonsai will tolerate slightly lower temperatures for very short periods. Summer temperatures between 16–18°C (61–64°F) should be maintained as far as possible.
Watering   Every day during the summer, every two to three days during the winter.
Propagation   Take semi-ripe cuttings in July

and place in a cold frame or glasshouse. Use compost Code 2 and bottom heat with a temperature between 16–18°C (61–64°F).
Compost   Code 4.
Root prune   Every year up to five then every two years.
Pest   Mainly free.
Disease   Mainly free.

ORANGE (*Citrus mitis*)

This small orange tree from the Philippines will make an excellent flowering indoor bonsai and if grown as a large specimen it will also make a good fruiting bonsai. For the beginner it is best to grow it as a simple flowering bonsai. The flowers are white and very fragrant, which adds to its beauty when grown in a conservatory.

Position   Plenty of light and sun, but keep in shade on very hot, sunny days. Good ventilation, frost-free room.
Temperature   Never allow the winter temperature to drop below 13°C (55°F). Summer temperature between 18–21°C (64–70°F).
Watering   Every day during the summer, every two to three days during the winter.
Propagation   Seed or cutting.
Seed   Sow seed in March in compost Code 1 at a temperature of 16°C (61°F).
Cuttings   Take semi-ripe cuttings between the months of July and August. Place in compost Code 2 with a bottom heat temperature of 18°C (64°F).
Compost   Code 4.
Root prune   Every two years up to four then every three years.
Pest   Mealybug.
Disease   Mainly free.

Fig 87   Opposite Orange. *Used as a bonsai but trained for its fruit instead of its tree-like shape.*

PARLOUR PALM
(*Chamaedorea elegans*)

The parlour palm is quite a common house plant and can be found in most garden centres or flower shops. I have chosen this palm for its cheapness and availability, making it a good starter bonsai to practise on. *See* section on growing in tufa (page 103).

Position   Allow for plenty of light and ventilation.
Temperature   All year round temperature between 10–22°C (50–72°F).
Watering   Every day during the summer, every day during the winter if grown over rock or in tufa – if grown in pot, every two to three days.
Propagation   It is less costly and time-consuming for the beginner to purchase a palm from garden centres or florist shops.
Compost   Code 4.
Root prune   Every three years if grown in a pot, no root pruning if grown in tufa.
Pest   Red spider mite.
Disease   Mildew.

PISTACHIO (*Pistacia*)

The pistachio is an evergreen cold room indoor bonsai with pinnate leaves and red fruits which are formed during the autumn.

Position   A cool room with plenty of ventilation and light.
Temperature   Summer temperature between

Fig 88   A young pistachio such as this one needs cold room conditions.

10–18°C (50–64°F), winter temperature should not fall below 10°C (50°F).

Watering   Every day during a warm summer, every two to three days during the winter.

Propagation   Seed or cuttings.

Compost   Code 4.

Root prune   Every year up to five then every two or three years depending on rate of growth.

Pest   Mainly free.

Disease   Mainly free.

POMEGRANATE
(*Punica granatum*)

An excellent small deciduous tree from Iran for indoor bonsai and suitable for either a cold or warm room. The flowers on the pomegranate are scarlet and tubular in shape, showing themselves during the months between June and September.

POMEGRANATE
(*Punica granatum 'Nana'*)

Smaller in size, flower and fruit, making it more suitable to grow as a bonsai than *Punica granatum*. As stated above, the pomegranate is a deciduous tree (one which loses its leaves) and will therefore need a rest period during the winter months. However, first-time buyers and beginners to the art of bonsai treat the tree as an evergreen which can lead to problems because of the tree's internal time clock.

Because you may find pomegranates that have been forced commercially and on sale all year round, this does not mean they are evergreen. Through tests I have carried out over the past few years, I have found the pomegranate will tolerate these conditions, but only for a two-year period, when it will then need to be placed into dormancy for a winter period.

The symptoms shown by the tree during the autumn and parts of the winter are three-fold:

1   The tree may drop some or all of its leaves and then shoot new ones.
2   Leaves tend to look sick and dull.
3   The tree starts to flower.

During the autumn and winter, therefore, the tree will need a constant level of light, and a controlled temperature as outlined on page 114, ventilation and watering as shown below. All these factors will help the tree to photosynthesise and produce sugar and starch. A feeding programme of a balanced fertiliser every month, alternating with a tomato feed, will help the tree through the winter period. The temperature needed for dormancy is given below.

Position   Plenty of light and full sun. Good ventilation at all times. Water well during the growing season in the summer, but only keep the compost moist during the winter.

Fig 89(a)   Pomegranate starting to flower.

83

Fig 89(b) *Pomegranate in full flower.*

Temperature Winter temperature can drop to 7°C (45°F) to allow the tree to drop its foliage. Summer temperature between 18–21°C (64–70°F). In dormancy keep the tree at a temperature of 7°C (45°F) from October through to March. Keep in total frost-free conditions.

Watering Every day during the summer, every two to three days during the winter.

Propagation Seed and cuttings.

Seed Seeds are sown in March in compost Code 1 between a temperature of 16–18°C (61–64°F).

Cuttings Take semi-ripe cuttings with a heel of between 7.5–9cm (3–3½in) long during the latter part of July to the beginning of August. Place in compost Code 2, with a bottom heat temperature of 16–18°C (61–64°F).

Compost Code 4.

Root prune Every year up to five, then every two years.

Pest Mainly free.

Disease Mainly free.

SAGERETIA (*Sageretia theezans*)

An evergreen tree from southern China with an interesting bark which flakes. The trunk will thicken in time.

Position As much light as possible. Misting is very beneficial.

Temperature Between 12–64°C (54–75°F).

Watering Every day during the summer, every two to three days during the winter.

Compost Code 4.

Propagation Cuttings, soft and semi-ripe.

Pest Mainly free.

Disease Mainly free.

SAGO PALM (*Cycas revoluta*)

The sago is grown as an artistic bonsai and could easily be confused with a glorified house plant.

Fig 90 Young sago palm seedling and seed.

As a bonsai, the sago expresses itself best when grown over or planted into volcanic rock, which is then placed on a flat bonsai dish without drainage holes and filled with water. Another way of displaying the sago is in a deep pot similar to the type used for cascade plantings and should have artistic Japanese or Chinese markings on it.

Position Sun or part shade.

Temperature Winter temperature should never fall below 10°C (50°F). Summer temperature between 16–18°C (61–64°F).

Watering Every day during the summer. For those planted in volcanic rock or tufa you may need to water twice a day.

Propagation Seed sown between February and April in compost Code 1 with a temperature of 24°C (75°F). Due to the size of the seed, use a deep seed tray or pot.

Suckers Remove suckers during April and May and place into compost Code 4.

Compost Code 4.

Root prune Every three years. May be troublesome. When grown in a rock no root pruning is required.

Pest Red spider mite.

Disease Mainly free.

Fig 91   Three serissas with interesting white trunks. The flowers are small and white.

SERISSA – Tree of a Thousand Stars (*Serissa foetida*)

A small-leaved tree from southern China and south-east Asia with a whitish trunk and white flowers.

Position   As much light as possible, but not direct sunlight. Try to minimise moving the tree from one position to another.
Temperature   Keep the temperature between 10–18°C (50–64°F).
Watering   Every day and sometimes twice a day during the summer. Do not over-water, but keep the compost moist. Winter, every one to two days depending on temperature.
Propagation   Cuttings, softwood and semi-ripe.
Compost   Code 4.
Root prune   Every two years up to six, then every two to three years depending on rate of growth.
Pest   Mainly free.
Disease   Die-back and yellow leaves. Keep movement of the tree to a minimum, give as much light as possible, but remove from glass areas during frost periods. Never allow the compost to become too dry.

SYDNEY GOLDEN WATTLE
(*Acacia longifolia*)

Another small, shrubby Australian tree known by its common name of 'Sydney Golden Wattle'. Again, as with the other acacias, the flowers are yellow, covering its dense network of branches, but this time strongly scented.

Position   Plenty of light and good ventilation.
Temperature   Winter – never allow the temperature to drop below 4°C (39°F). Summer temperature between 15–18°C (59–64°F).
Watering   Every day during the summer, every two to three days during the winter.

Propagation   Seed or cuttings.
Seed   Sow seeds in April in compost Code 1 at a temperature of 16°C (61°F).
Cuttings   Young and semi-ripe cuttings with a heel taken between the months of April and May in a compost Code 2 at a temperature between 16–18°C (61–64°F).
Compost   Code 4, extra sand.
Root prune   Every year up to five, then every two years.
Pest   Mealybug.
Disease   Mainly free.

Fig 92   The type of seedling the beginner should be looking for.

CHAPTER 7

Group Plantings

Groups can be placed in four different categories: true groups; landscapes; raft plantings; and multiple trunk. This classification takes away the confusion between the four. For example, the raft plant, which I will cover in more detail later, is grown from a main layered trunk containing one root system, whereas the true group plantings are all individual trees, each with their own root system. The multiple trunks which are sometimes confused for a group planting have a single root system and one main upright trunk from which the other five or more trunks extend. Landscapes can be either individual

Fig 93   Small landscape with two serissas.

trees or a raft, but the difference between the group and landscape is that for the latter, rocks, miniature houses, water and small oriental figures are used to help create the illusion of a scenic view.

TRUE GROUP

As stated before, this is a group of individual trees placed into a single tray all with their own root system. The advantage of such a group is that if one tree is damaged or becomes diseased it is easier to replace that tree without removing the complete group from its dish.

Before you start to draw a first and second dimensional plan as described previously, you must understand one of the basic rules when trying to create an optical illusion – always place the tallest tree at the front of the group. By doing this you will give a feeling of depth as the trees at

Fig 94   The basic items used in making the landscape shown in Fig 93.

Fig 95 Two ways of creating an optical illusion of depth – planting a tall tree in the centre, and using a shallow dish.

Fig 96 Dishes suitable for group and landscape plantings.

the back seem to be further away when shown on a smaller scale, as in Fig 95.

There is, however, one exception to the rule and that is to place one very tall tree in the centre of a group and surround it by small trees descending in height as they reach the rim of the dish, as in Fig 95.

Dishes

The dish is an important factor to consider. By this I mean the size, shape and depth will play its part in adding to the optical illusion. As shown in Fig 96 there are two dishes suitable for group plantings. The large brown dish has a wide, flat rim, which when planted hides the depth and is therefore beneficial because it allows the root system to grow. The small dish has a very thin rim, but will still give the same optical illusion because of its shallowness. However, the root systems of the trees planted in the shallow dish will need to be of a more fibrous nature than for those planted in the larger style.

Step one   Start by drawing a first and second dimensional plan and then add notes to your plan, such as type of trees, the temperature of the room they are to be kept in, and how much light is available – will it be sufficient or will you need to substitute more light in the form of grow lights? When all this information has been compiled it will help you to pick the right seedling for your group planting.

Fig 97 Forming a canopy. All trunks should be in full view and shown as individuals, but coming together to form a single canopy with top growth.

Step two Once you have drawn two circles showing height, width, depth and angles, pencil in the dish. Follow this by pencilling in the trunks and their angles. Most of the angles shown are between 90 degrees in the middle of the group down to 45 degrees at the two sides of the group. It is important at this stage to try to show all the trunks. Do not hide one trunk behind the other. Now pencil in the side and sub-lateral side branches, keeping them as individuals, but at the same time giving consideration to forming one complete canopy over the entire group, as in Fig 97.

Step three When you have finished drawing your plans and have decided on the variety and the number of trees to be used to create the group (which should all be two-year-old pruned seedlings where possible), start by building a framework to wire the trees into their respective positions as indicated on your plan.

As shown, the frame is made of thin bamboo canes woven together and shaped by cutting the ends of the canes to fit the dish. The frame is then anchored down by wire through the drainage holes, first covering the holes with green mesh, then pushing the wire through the mesh. Anchor more wire to the bamboo frame

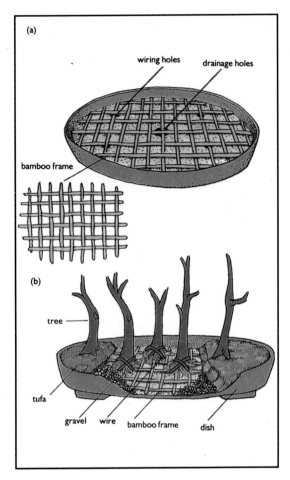

Fig 98 (a) and (b) By using a bamboo frame trees may be planted in any position in the dish.

as close as possible to where the tree's root system will sit. This is followed by adding the 6mm drainage gravel to the bottom of the dish as in Fig 98 (a). The trees are not wired through the drainage holes, but to the frame only (Fig 98 (b)).

Step four Place a thin layer of compost on top of the drainage gravel (the compost code will depend on the type of tree), then position the trees. Once you have placed and angled all the trees, with the tallest at the front, shortest at the back and sides, fill in with fresh compost, working it skilfully between the tree's root

Fig 99 (a) Landscape – seven serissas placed in a long oblong dish. Figures, stones and pathways add to the illusion.

system. Washed 4mm gravel may be spread over the surface of the compost if you wish, which will help to keep the neck of the trees clean, stop the surface of the compost from drying out too quickly and help to control any weeds that may start to grow if the tree is placed outside during the warm, sunny days of summer.

Step five Continue to prune and shape the top and side growth until you have reached your chosen shape, pruning back new growth. This will become a seasonal practice.

Aftercare Follow a feeding, watering and spraying programme throughout the year.

LANDSCAPE

The landscape may also use individual trees in the same way as the true group shown above but rocks, a pathway and an old Chinese figure will give the impression of a tranquil landscape.

Step one Follow the same procedure as for groups, by drawing a plan and making notes on type of tree, height, width and dish. In the photograph above I have used a long, shallow dish, but other shapes could be used, such as a kidney dish as in Fig 99 (b). Once you have finished your plan and chosen your seedlings, build a bamboo frame as shown in the landscape

Fig 99 (b)   Landscape – two myrtles placed in a kidney-shaped pot with a section especially made to hold water.

section. Wire this to the tray and then, using more wire, fasten it to the bamboo, coming as close to the base of the individual trees as possible. Spread a layer of 6mm gravel for drainage, followed by a thin layer of compost, then place and wire your trees into their position as shown on your plan. Continue to work more fresh compost into and around the root system until you reach just below the rim of the dish.

When you re-pot you should normally leave a small space between the compost and the top of the pot. This allows for watering without washing the compost away, but with the landscape and the groups you will need to form mounds of compost at certain points to add to the illusion of an uneven terrain.

Between these mounds, spread a thin line of 4mm gravel, making the line wider at the front of the tray and narrower at the back. Rocks, if used, should form a single line, with all the contours facing the same way. Although they may be individual pieces, try to make them look like one cliff or mountain side. You may if you wish add moss to the mounds and allow it to grow, but it is very important that you keep checking for pests which may hide under the moss.

Step two Continue to prune and shape each tree as you would for an individual tree, but at the same time blend each one so that the foliage canopy forms into one unit. Try to avoid too many crossing branches.

Aftercare Follow a feeding, watering and spraying programme throughout the year.

RAFT

The raft is a continuous trunk placed on its side and the side branches allowed to grow and thicken as if they were individual trees, as in Fig 100.

Step one There are two ways of forming a raft. The first is to place an indoor seedling on its side, on a bench in a heated glasshouse ideally. Indoor growing is possible with a makeshift table top or shelf as in Fig 101 (a).

By placing the seedling on its side you allow the light to work for you by pulling those branches facing downwards back up towards the light source as shown in the line drawing.

Continue to shape each branch as if it was an individual trunk. The sub-lateral growth from these side branches, or 'trunks' as they are now termed, should be treated as side branches. The top of each new trunk should form into a canopy giving the illusion of a woodland or forest setting. To water you will need to remove the side of the pot facing upward.

Step two When the branches have responded to the pull of light and the sub-lateral

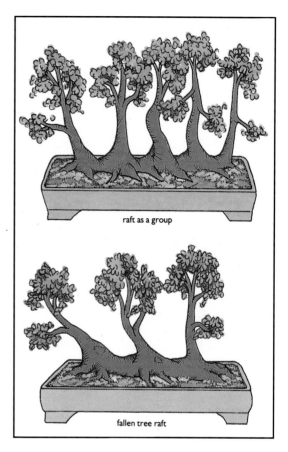

raft as a group

fallen tree raft

Fig 100   The raft. This creates the illusion of a clump of trees, or gives the impression of a fallen tree which has taken root.

side shoots have turned woody, this is the time to transplant the seedling into a training pot. The pot can be made from wood or plastic, or be boat-shaped as shown in Fig 102.

Whichever type of pot is used you will have the problem of covering the large root ball at one end. This can be overcome in two ways. The first is to fill your training pot with gravel for drainage in the normal manner. Add compost to form a hollow where the root ball will be positioned by filling to the level of one-third of the pot. The rest of the pot should be filled as normal.

The other way to hide the root ball is to use a

93

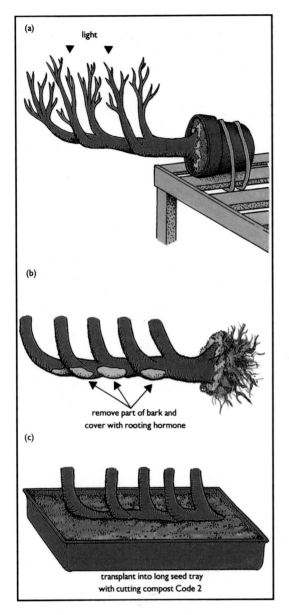

(a)

light

(b)

remove part of bark and
cover with rooting hormone

(c)

transplant into long seed tray
with cutting compost Code 2

*Fig 101 (a) to (c)   Seedling tied to the top of the bench,
allowing light to change the direction of branch
growth.*

*Fig 102   Two containers suitable for starting
a raft.*

undercut the main trunk running horizontally along the compost to expose the cambium. Apply rooting hormone to the cuts and pin the main trunk with wire to the surface of the compost. In time a root system will develop from each of the cuts which will link up with the first root ball. It would then be possible to remove one-half of the first root ball, allowing the raft to be repotted into a flat dish at the next root pruning session.

RAFT FROM LAYERING

The other way to produce a raft is to layer. This is when a branch from the chosen plant material is pinned to the surface of the compost and roots are allowed to form on the underside of the branch, as in Fig 103.

Step one   Start by choosing a non-flowering branch, from which all growth is removed from the underside. With a knife, remove sections of the bark from the underside of the branch as in Fig 101 (b). Cover the wounds with a rooting hormone and then pin the branch carefully to

boat-shaped pot which has a higher point at one end. This is ideal for sitting the root ball in, and allows the compost to be graded on a slope.

Whichever way you choose, you will have to

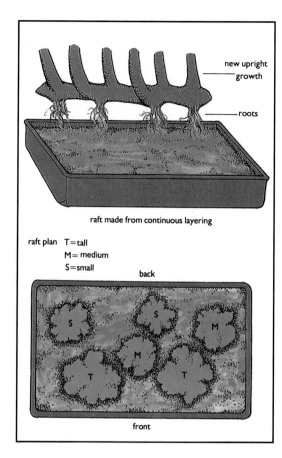

raft made from continuous layering

raft plan T = tall
          M = medium
          S = small

Fig 103   A plan should be sketched out to guide you.

and second dimensional plan as demonstrated at the beginning of this chapter. Follow a feeding, watering and spraying for pest and disease programme throughout the year.

MULTIPLE TRUNKS

Basically this is a single tree and is not really in the same category as groups, but when the style has a very short base trunk with a thick surface root some people confuse it with either a raft or a compact group, which is the reason I have added this style to a chapter on groups.

Step one   To produce such a tree you first need a seedling with very low bud growth. Once you have found such a seedling, either from seed, cutting or purchased from a nursery, begin by drawing your plan and deciding how many trunks you would like, remembering to keep to three, five or seven. When you have finished your plan remove all the top growth down to three buds, allowing these buds to develop until

the surface of the compost. Roots should develop from the wounded areas within a few months. Whilst you are waiting for the root system to form, continue to prune and shape those branches which will form the upright trunks to the raft, as shown in Fig 101 (c).

Step two   Once the root system has formed and gained strength, remove by cutting away from the mother tree, remembering to cover both the end of the raft and the wound on the mother tree with a sealant containing a fungicide.

Aftercare   Continue to shape the raft as you would for the true group and follow your first

Fig 104   The multiple trunk bonsai grows from one root base.

they have produced more buds at the bottom of the new growth. Choose two of the lowest, outward facing buds on the new growth and cut back as before. All other buds and new growth should be removed.

Step two   Allow these buds to grow until they have reached the height at which the side branches will start, then shape to the design of your plan. The trunks which are in the centre of the group of trunks should be allowed to grow taller than those on the outside. Avoid too many crossing branches in the centre of the group and form a balance of top growth.

Aftercare   Follow a feeding, watering and spraying for pest and disease programme throughout the year.

Fig 105   Young serissa, showing its white trunk.

CHAPTER 8

Rock Plantings

The rock planting for the indoor bonsai is basically the same as the hardy outdoor bonsai, but we are able to add more grace and charm with decorative pots, small glazed figures and less hardy rock such as tufa. With the artificial conditions we are able to expose the roots slightly more than a tree which has to contend with strong winds and heavy rainfall.

ROCKS

It would be true to say that the shape of the rock will make all the difference to the final appearance of the rock planting and therefore in most cases the rock is chosen before the tree. I always keep a stock of trees with a suitable root system for growing over, on, or in rocks and then, when

Fig 106   Pomegranate straddling a rock and starting to flower.

Fig 107   Volcanic rock can be made to look
attractive in a variety of ways.

I am able to find a suitable rock, it is just a case of choosing the right shape of root system to fit the rock. At the same time I try as far as possible to choose a seedling that has the style I am looking for. However, this is not so important at this stage, because the tree can be shaped by pruning to buds, wiring and removing unwanted branches at a later period.

Volcanic Rock

This rock, which is usually imported from Japan, is far superior to most other forms of rock. When treated, several different colours of white, grey and sometimes green may be seen and even without a tree planted in them, they can be both artistic and peaceful-looking, as in Fig 107.

Volcanic rock is a very hard material and therefore you will need a drill and chisel when constructing root and drainage channels.

Note Children should have an adult to supervise the use of tools and especially those which use electricity. Adults should also remember to unwind the electric cable on the drill to its full extent to stop the cable from over heating, and always work away from wet areas. Some form of eye protection is advisable when chipping stone.

Tufa

This is a very soft, porous rock and quite suitable for indoor bonsai. Because the tufa is so soft, forming holes for the root system to fit into is a simple task. The disadvantage is that it may only last between ten and fifteen years depending on the growth of the root system through the tufa.

Thermal Block

Many of the bonsai clubs in England are now experimenting with thermal block and the reason for this is the easy way in which it can be shaped. However, this is not a very clean job and

Fig 108   Making a hollow in a piece of tufa is an easy task.

therefore I would advise using old clothes and a face mask.

STYLES

There are four ways to assemble a rock planting – root over rock, root planted in rock, root planted on to rock and root by the side of rock.

Root over Rock

Step one   First you must find a suitable rock, such as a rock which has an arrowhead shape, an area to sit the V–shape of a root system (imitating a person straddling a horse, as shown in Fig 109).

The seedling shown in the photograph was chosen in its second year and instead of root pruning in the normal way, two large woody roots were chosen to form the V–shape. The

99

Fig 109 *A young pomegranate straddling a piece of volcanic rock.*

Fig 110 *Roots exposed over a rock can give a good aged appearance to the tree.*

rest of the large woody roots were removed, and the fibrous roots with their fine root hairs were encouraged to develop in length by holding the neck of the root ball at the top of a tall, slim pot and growing in a sandy compost such as Code 2, which was gently worked in, filling the empty spaces around and in between the root system.

Because of the compost mixture of Code 2 (sand and moss peat, basically a cutting mix, therefore low in nutrients), a careful feeding programme has to be followed throughout the complete year.

Start by drawing a first and second dimension plan of your rock planting. Make notes of type of tree, its growing habits and likes and dislikes such as temperature and light. Once this is done, choose your seedling carefully and follow the root pruning procedure as shown in Fig 111. Continue to shape the top of the tree as normal

by following your plan. This process should be carried out for the next two to four years, depending on the root system.

Step two When you are satisfied that the root has developed sufficiently, that is to say there are two long, woody roots and an abundance of small, finer roots, then at the right time of the year (March), remove the tree from its training pot. By gently pulling the roots apart, place them over the top of the piece of rock you chose at the start. Trying not to damage any roots, gently push a few of the fibrous roots into the grooves of the rock, starting at the top and working down to the bottom of the rock. Once you have reached the bottom, tie the root system into the base of the rock as shown in Fig 111 (c).

Place the tree into a tall training pot or plastic pot with a good drainage system at the bottom. Do not prune the root for the next three to four years, except for cutting away the top one-third of the pipe or pot and removing the soil from the roots around this area. This will leave one-third of the top section of the roots exposed, which in time will turn woody and take on an aged appearance. Follow the same procedure for the next two years, each time removing one-third of the training pot, until with the removal of the last

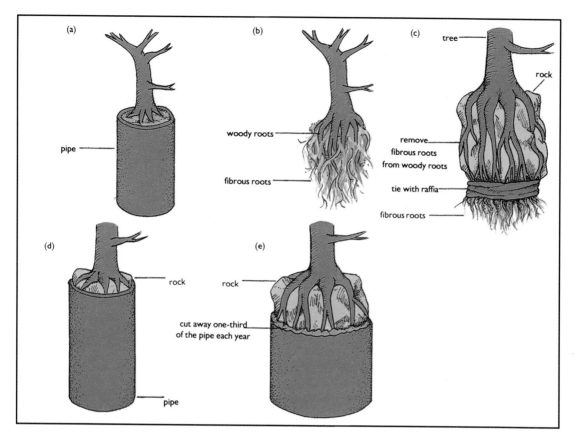

(a)

pipe

(b)

woody roots

fibrous roots

(c)

tree

rock

remove
fibrous roots
from woody roots

tie with raffia

fibrous roots

(d)

rock

pipe

(e)

rock

cut away one-third
of the pipe each year

*Fig 111   The roots which are exposed to the air will gradually turn woody
and expand in the crevice of rock. These will hold the tree in place.*

section of pot, remove one-third of the root at the bottom of the stone (the root ball below the stone area), as you would for normal root pruning.

Plant on to Rock

Volcanic rock or an interesting piece of rock found in England will be best suited to this construction. Tufa will not hold the pins without some form of glue, which may spread into this porous rock. You will need a drill and several sizes of masonry bits, a small chisel and a wooden mallet to prepare the rock for planting.

Step one   Find a piece of rock, with a flat base if possible, then draw a two-dimensional plan of the illusion you wish to create, not forgetting to make notes of the type of tree or trees,

temperature range, likes and dislikes and the light factor.

Commence by marking and drilling four holes ready for the pins, the depth of the holes depending on the length of the pins and the hardness of the rock (*see* Fig 114). Try as far as possible to drill the holes slightly smaller than the diameter of the pin, thereby forcing the pin into the hole. This avoids glueing, which does not create a problem in hardy non-porous rock, but may do so in tufa, as already stated.

Step two   When you have drilled the four holes, drill a larger hole for drainage in the centre of the four holes from the top of the rock to the bottom. Because of the hardness of the rock this is not always possible. It may crack when a hole is drilled, but this is far better than allowing water to flow down the side of the rock, damaging

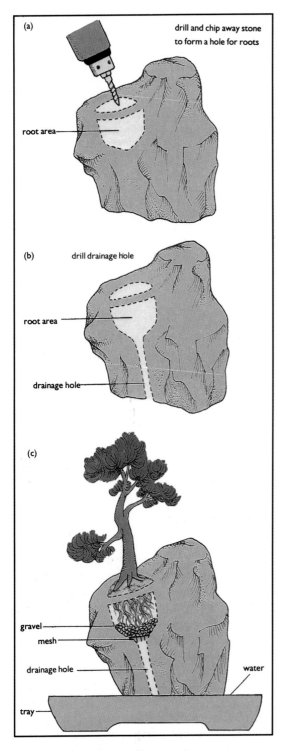

Fig 112   Planting young trees in rock. Gravel and mesh will prevent the compost from blocking the drainage hole you have drilled.

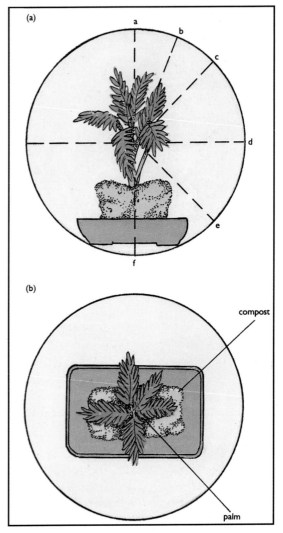

Fig 113   A palm in tufa. (a) First dimensional plan. (b) Second dimensional plan.

other plantings of trees or small ground-cover alpine-type mosses.

Step three   When you have secured the pins to the rock, cover the centre drainage hole with a piece of mesh. This prevents the compost blocking the drainage hole. Now place the tree in position and secure to the rock by running thin training wire from one pin across to the next.

Step four   Now use a compost mix of 50 per cent moss peat, 25 per cent seed compost, 15

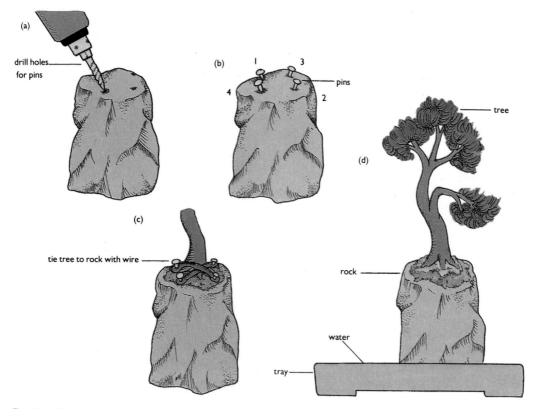

Fig 114   *Pinning a tree to a rock can be quite simple. Care should be taken never to allow the compost to dry out.*

per cent sharp sand, 10 per cent sphagnum moss. Work this mixture into and around the root system and cover with a fine hair-net or similar. Once you have completed all the above, place the tree and rock (providing you have used a rock with a flat base) on to a humidity tray without drainage holes. This will be far better than a pot, because it will help with the humidity indoors, and it will enable you to display the rock and tree with more grace.

Gently water the compost and keep a regular check to stop it from drying out. Do not feed the root system for one month. Instead use a foliage feed until the second month when a normal feeding programme should be followed. Feeding is a very important factor with this type of planting.

Step five   Continue to shape the top of the tree, keeping to your plan as far as possible. Root pruning will only take place if and when the root system extends to the chosen root area, but you might find the roots are slow to develop on rock.

Root in Rock (Tufa)

For this example I will use tufa and a palm, both of which should be available from most garden centres. The palm I have chosen is the parlour palm (*Chamaedorea elegans*), firstly because it has been a tried and tested house plant by many people, and secondly because with a little imagination, time, a humidity tray and piece of tufa it can make an attractive indoor bonsai.

Step one   Again, first draw your first and second dimensional plan. Remember to make notes on the type of tree, temperature and light factor. This may seem unimportant at the time, but as your collection starts to build, planning for the tree's placement with the right amount of light and temperature is an important factor.

103

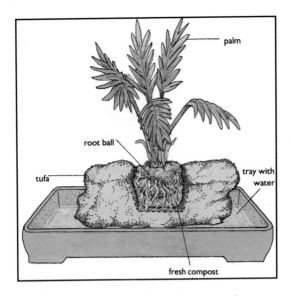

Fig 115   Forming a hole in tufa is quite an easy task.

Fig 116   A young Jacqueline elm seedling planted so that it will eventually grow through the centre of the volcanic rock.

Step two   If you have not mastered the art of propagation, purchase the palm from your local garden centre. Those who feel confident can grow from seed, also purchased at your local garden centre or bonsai centre. First remove the palm from its pot and look at the size of the root system (width and depth) as this will give you some indication of the width, depth and shape of hole to carve in the tufa. Because of its porous nature, there is no need for a drainage hole in tufa, as moisture will travel by capillary action (downwards, upwards and sideways).

Step three   Using a chisel, carve a hole slightly bigger than the root system, then spread a small amount of compost Code 3 at the bottom of the hole as shown in Fig 115. Place the root ball into the hole and fill in between and around the root system with more compost Code 3, almost to the top of the hole, allowing a small gap from the compost level to the top of the hole to prevent water from washing away the compost. Once the root system becomes established, it will work its way in to the tufa, anchoring the palm to the tufa.

Aftercare   The palm will need watering every two to four days, depending on room temperature and type of heating. Feed once a month with a general fertiliser containing N:7 P:7 K:7, plus trace elements, throughout the year. Pruning consists of pulling off old, dead foliage and removing any new tall growths to keep the foliage compact and force out new shoots lower down. To control pests such as red spider mite, *see* page 110. Use a humidity tray filled with water which, unlike placing a pot into a tray full of water which would stop the circulation of air and hinder the drainage, allows the air to flow around the roots in the tufa.

There are other ways of planting a tree into rock, such as the system used in the landscape plantings. I have used artificially constructed pieces of rock to hold a tree or trees in Fig 117. This is just a simple case of using the pocket or pockets in the piece of rock as you would with a pot by first placing mesh over the drainage hole, covering the mesh with 6mm gravel and adding more fresh compost to the root ball when in position.

Fig 117   Four stages of a palm tree.

Growing Next to Rock

This type of planting, although very simple to achieve, will take a little artistic ability and foresight, but having said that the construction side is very simple. The potting is basically the same as potting an individual tree except that you place a piece of rock next to it. The difficult part is finding a tree and rock that will balance and show some form of artistic harmony when placed together.

CHAPTER 9

Pests and Diseases

This is probably the hardest aspect for the new grower to understand. I say this because there are so many more different causes to problems, such as yellow leaves, brown leaves, tips turning black, that the beginner can be thrown into a state of confusion. However, by following a spraying programme for both pest and disease you will help to eliminate some of the problems.

Fig 118   A dead pine, killed through being placed on top of a television and being attacked by red spider mite.

IMPORTED TREES

Government regulations in Britain state that trees and shrubs imported from certain parts of the world cannot enter the country without first obtaining a certificate of health from the country of origin. Trees from countries outside the European Community, such as Japan, will need to be placed in isolation on arrival in Britain.

The area for keeping trees in isolation is first inspected by a qualified plant health official from the ministry who, after an inspection of the site, will visit when the trees arrive, and several times after, to inspect them for signs of pest or disease. Many people when on holiday abroad are unaware of such rules, and if told, class them as being no more than government red-tape. These rules are anything but red-tape, and without strict import controls Britain could be overrun with new strains of pest and disease.

However, some trees do find their way into the country in shopping-bags, suitcases and via black market activities. I cannot stress enough to the bonsai grower the importance of not purchasing such a tree. Although you can see no signs of pest or disease, this does not mean there are none and with such a tree you are taking the risk of either losing your complete bonsai collection or destroying other plants growing indoors. Also, it could be the cause of the loss of thousands of outside plants such as fruit trees through a new strain of pest or disease spreading, and at the same time you would be risking serious trouble with the authorities.

Fig 119 Olive tree losing its leaves through being placed in a high temperature.

HYGIENE

Hygiene plays a very important part in the control of pests and diseases. Dead leaves, off-cuts from pruning, old soil all help to increase pest and disease problems. Always burn, and never compost, diseased foliage and wood. Tools should be kept clean, and be sterilised after pruning a diseased bonsai. Old pots and dishes should be washed before using again. Old compost that has contained a diseased or pest-infected bonsai should be thrown away. By following basic hygiene rules such as these you will help to control the spread of pests and diseases.

CHEMICAL SPRAYS

Today there is a wide range of insecticides and fungicides on the garden centres' shelves. Many are similar in content and will work as well as the next, but there are a few specially designed for a particular insect or disease. To give brand names is almost impossible because by the time it would take to test all the sprays on the market, most of them would have been out-dated by new chemicals.

The answer is first to identify the pest or disease, then to ask for advice at your local garden centre, which should be able to supply you either with a general spray that will cover most pests and diseases, or with one which will control your individual problem. For most indoor sprays they will offer an aerosol, which will give you less control over the strength of the chemical you wish to use. If possible try to purchase a bottle or packet which will enable you to make your own mixture and decide on the strength you wish to use. In most cases the bought spray is slightly under the recommendation shown on a bottle or packet.

Mixing Sprays

Never mix two chemicals unless it states on the container which chemicals are compatible. Never follow one spray with another without first washing the sprayer through with clean water. Not only will mixing the wrong combination of chemicals together become toxic and dangerous to yourself, it may also damage the foliage on your bonsai, and could even cause the death of the tree.

There are two kinds of chemical sprays, contact spray which works on the outside of the bonsai, and systemic which works on the inside. Contact sprays stick to the surface of the foliage killing anything which lands there whilst systemic sprays circulate in the sap of the bonsai and kill insects which feed on the tree. Watering can wash away the contact, and therefore the need to spray is more frequent, whereas the systemic is inside the bonsai and it should last longer, cutting down use.

Before attempting to use the spray, check the instructions for plants suitable for spraying and

107

take notice of other warnings, such as 'do not eat or drink when spraying'. Those keeping fish should check if spray is harmful to fish. All children should have supervision when using chemicals, and always keep chemicals away from children and pets. Always wear rubber gloves when spraying, and wash your hands afterwards. Never place chemicals in unmarked containers.

FLOWERING AND FRUITING BONSAI

Never spray your bonsai with an insecticide or fungicide during the flowering season for fear of harming helpful insects such as bees.

INSECTS

Although this book is written for the indoor bonsai grower, I feel that I should also mention some of the outdoor insects, aphids and caterpillars being the most likely to attack indoor bonsai when placed outside during the warm days of summer.

Glasshouse Aphid (*Aulacorthum solani*)

Yellow to green in colour. This aphid feeds on the young foliage of many types of indoor, cold room and outdoor bonsai during a warm summer.

Control For bonsai such as some forms of prunus used as cold room trees, alternate spraying with contact and systemic insecticides throughout the spraying programme. Smoke glasshouses and cold frames to kill over-wintering eggs before the start of the season.

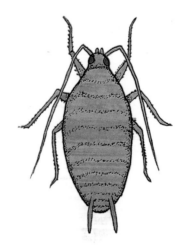

Fig 120   An aphid.

Green Apple Aphid (*Aphis pomi*)

A troublesome aphid which attacks flowering and fruiting bonsai, feeding on their foliage, buds and parts of the blossom which in turn affect the fruits.

Control Read through 'Flowering and Fruiting' above. Before and after flowering, alternate between a systemic and contact insecticide.

Peach Aphid (*Myzus persicae*)

This aphid can be more troublesome than most other forms, attacking bonsai palm trees and a wide range of other indoor bonsai. The colour of peach aphid is yellow to green and in some cases mixed pink-yellow to green.

Control Kill over-wintering eggs in glasshouses with smoke. Use contact or systemic spray in your spraying programme.

Privet Aphid (*Myzus ligustri*)

With the use of privet in the bonsai world in recent years, the privet aphid should be added to our list. This has also been known as the privet leaf roller, because it rolls the leaves and feeds inside them, causing some bonsai to drop their foliage.

Control   Alternate spraying with a contact and systemic from spring onwards.

Spruce Aphid
(*Elatobium abietinum*)

This green aphid feeds on bonsai spruce and picea, causing the bonsai to turn yellow in colour.

Control   Alternate spraying with contact and systemic from the beginning of March.

Root Aphid

Several different forms of aphid, varying in colour from black to white, and some with a wax covering, will attack the root systems of indoor and cold room bonsai, but only on the odd occasion have I found them on outdoor bonsai. Attack from the root aphid may cause the bonsai to wilt or look unsightly.

Control   Looking at the root system when root pruning will keep a check on this aphid and if discovered you should follow the procedure as shown below:

1   Remove all the compost from the root system by gently flushing with clean water.
2   Spray the entire root system with a contact insecticide.
3   Re-pot without root pruning in fresh compost to allow the roots to recover.

Sycamore Aphid
(*Drepanosiphum platanidis*)

This green and fairly large aphid attacks the bonsai maple, feeding on the buds and foliage.

Control   Spray with a systemic insecticide as buds start to open, then spray with a forceful jet

of clean, soapy water twice a week. Remove dead insects by hand.

Willow Aphid
(*Tuberolachnus salignus*)

Very large, brown aphid which feeds on the woody section of bonsai willows.

Control   Spray from May onwards, alternating between a contact and systemic insecticide.

Woolly Aphid
(*Eriosoma lanigerum*)

This brown aphid, which covers itself in a white, woolly wax, can be a serious threat to bonsai growers. It feeds on the fine, twiggy branches of several types of bonsai, especially the flowering and fruiting varieties.

Control   Follow a spraying programme, using contact and systemic insecticide. Remove by hand with cotton bud and white spirit.

Mealybug
(*Pseudococcus obscurus*)

The mealybug will attack indoor, cold room and, in very warm summers, hardy outdoor bonsai. The mealybug, which is recognised by its white-waxy covering, attacks the bonsai, weakening it and therefore rendering it unsuitable for bonsai training. Most mealybugs are found on the bonsai's branches and trunk, but on occasions they will also infest the root system.

Control   Mealybug survive best in a warm temperature, therefore ventilate well to keep temperatures down. Removing by hand with a cotton bud covered with methylated spirit is the best way of destroying this pest. Isolate any bonsai found with mealybug until the bonsai is completely free from the pest. Follow a spraying programme, alternating between contact and systemic insecticide.

Conifer Mite
(*Oligonychus ununguis*)

This mite will attack bonsai from the beginning of the year onwards, causing it to turn yellow, and in some cases to drop its foliage. Indoor pine and other conifer-type bonsai can be seriously damaged by this mite.

Control   Start your spraying programme from the end of March, alternating between a contact and systemic insecticide.

Fruit Tree Red Spider Mite
(*Panonychus ulmi*)

This is the main, but not the only, red spider to attack fruiting bonsai such as peach.

Control   Follow a spraying programme using one of the chemicals for fruit red spider.

Red Spider Mite/Glasshouse
(*Tetranychus urticae* and
Tetranychus cinnabarinus)

These tiny mites attack many different types of indoor bonsai, covering their foliage with a very fine silk webbing, which may only be noticeable by looking down or across the leaf at eye level. The foliage is weakened by the mites' attack, causing it to change colour and die.

Control   Red spiders thrive in hot, dry conditions, therefore ventilate to control temperatures and spray bonsai with a fine mist of clean water once daily during warm periods. A humidity tray will help, but remember not to stand the bonsai in water. Follow a spraying programme throughout the year.

Note   Many beginners, when they first come across the term 'red spider mite', automatically think of a spider such as a smaller version of the

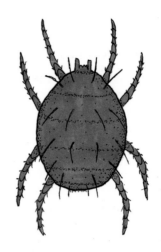

Fig 121   *The red spider mite.*

type found about the house. The mite was related to the spider a long time ago, but other than its speed of movement, you are looking for something different in shape, as shown in Fig 121.

Azalea Whitefly (*Pealius azaleae*)

A sticky honeydew and sooty mould is left by this pale green insect found on both the upper and lower surfaces of the foliage.

Control   Alternate with a contact and systemic insecticide.

Glasshouse Whitefly
(*Trialeurodes vaporariorum*)

Look for the sticky honeydew left by this insect, which can be found on both upper and lower surfaces of the foliage.

Control   Alternate between a contact and a systemic insecticide spray.

DISEASES

Grey Mould *(Botrytis cinerea)*

Grey mould can be found on seed trays, seedlings and woody sections of an older bonsai. *See* damping-off disease in the seed section, page 35.

Control   Do not over water seeds, seedlings or bonsai especially when temperatures are low. Always make sure there is a good drainage system at the bottom of the tray or pot being used. A good airflow will play a very important part in helping to control grey mould and this is why I always allow air into the centre of the seedling and mature tree by taking out crossing branches. Follow a spraying programme throughout the year, with a fungicide.

Fig 122   *Coral spot is a danger to indoor bonsai which are placed outside during the summer.*

Coral Spot (*Nectria cinnabarina*)

This fungus will chiefly attack outdoor bonsai. It is advisable for the indoor grower to understand a little about the disease, which attacks when the indoor bonsai is placed outside on warm days in summer.

Coral spot will cause die-back, and in most bonsai cases will kill the tree or cause the shape to be changed through essential drastic pruning measures. Once the bonsai has been attacked by this fungus you always live in fear of it returning and placing other bonsai at risk; therefore in bad cases it is probably best to destroy such a bonsai by burning. Coral spot is recognised by its salmon-pink coloured growths about the size of a pinhead, as shown in Fig 122.

Control/Prevention

1   Hygiene is the most important factor; never leave pruning wood lying about. Always keep a plastic bag to place the prunings in and then burn them at the first opportunity.
2   Check for old tree stumps in the garden close by. Cut, remove and burn any found. An old tree stump may look very nice covered with a climber or ground cover plant, but it may also cause the death of your prized bonsai. At the same time, check all old wooden objects for the fungus. I have found it on the bottom of back doors, especially old cottage-type buildings.
3   Always use fresh soil which is pest and disease free. Check the area used for mixing the soil, such as a wooden board. If there is any sign of coral spot, burn the board and find a replacement.
4   When pruning during the summer or winter, make sure the cuts are close to the joint and on an angle so that water will run away from the pruning cut. *See* pruning to a bud, page 44.
5   Always clean your pruning tool with methylated or surgical spirit before use. Paint all pruning cuts with a wound sealant directly after finishing the cut.
6   Check for the disease at the start of the year, especially during the spring, then use a systemic fungicide throughout the growing season.

Pruning is the best cure for this disease, but the cut should be several centimetres away from the diseased area, back into clean wood. Sometimes

Fig 123   Using clean soil and spraying with a
fungicide will help to control moulds.

the pruning may be so drastic you should
consider whether it is worth keeping the bonsai.

Damping-Off Disease

See damping-off, page 35.

Die-Back

Many bonsai suffer from die-back in one form or
another. I say that because the die-back may be
caused through fungi and bacteria which lead to
forms of canker, scale insects which also help to
introduce fungi into the bonsai, viruses, frost
damage, wind, bad pruning and many more,
adding to the confusion for the beginner. Therefore, as a general rule when coming across die-
back, look for a cause which may be other than
on or in the diseased bonsai. Make notes and use
the experience in the future. Prevention is
better than cure.

Control   As a general rule, remove diseased
branches, cutting back into clean wood. As soon
as the diseased part has been removed cover

Fig 124(a)   A pomegranate killed through bad
pruning.

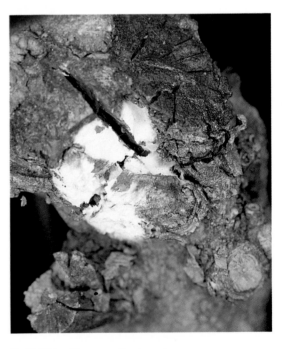

Fig 124(b)   Close-up of bad pruning.

the wound with a sealant containing a fungicide. Never keep the prunings; burn them or place them into a plastic bag until such time that burning is convenient, which should be no longer than a week. Follow a spraying programme using a fungicide throughout the growing season.

WEATHER CONDITIONS AND EFFECTS

The weather conditions shown below are directed to the beginner who wishes to grow indoor bonsai, but to place the tree outside during warm days in the summer, or for those who grow in glasshouse or conservatory environment which can be very beneficial for the tree when the conditions are right. Therefore, for those of you who only grow indoor bonsai, only the sections on temperature, light and frost should be taken into consideration.

Frost

All bonsai, whether hardy outdoor or the less hardy bonsai, will be severely damaged if attacked by frost, causing the young growth to turn black, or 'scorch' as it is termed. This may also lead to other diseases such as canker.

There are two kinds of frost, air frost and ground frost and the times they are at their most destructive are spring and autumn, with the spring frost being the most troublesome for those bonsai placed close to a window or grown in a glasshouse or conservatory.

Spring Frost

Although most indoor growers may think all frosts are the same, it is good practice to understand why the spring frost may cause more damage than the autumn frost, just in case you are tempted to place your tree outside too early. First look 'inside' the bonsai. In the section on wind it is explained how moisture moves inside the tree. Frost damage is caused by the

Fig 125(a)   Serissa damaged by frost due to the tree being left on a cold window sill overnight.

moisture inside the cell tissue of the bonsai turning into ice crystals. During the autumn when normal trees and shrubs enter a dormancy period, less and less moisture is therefore available to form these ice crystals, which also means that these trees and shrubs, and the hardy deciduous bonsai, are slowly introduced into the colder conditions of the winter months and therefore less damage is caused.

As most indoor bonsai are evergreen, with the exception of cold room bonsai such as Chinese water elm, Jacqueline elm and pomegranate (*see* page 65), sap is still conducting inside the tree, which means there is danger from frost. Therefore, all indoor bonsai should be moved indoors from August. Spring frosts are just the opposite, and therefore more damaging to normal trees, shrubs, hardy bonsai and deciduous indoor bonsai because they have more moisture to draw on. Therefore placement is a very important factor when the indoor bonsai has started conducting moisture to all parts of its structure. Spring frost attacks any time from the beginning of March until the beginning of May and it is at this time when buds, new shoots and juvenile foliage run the highest risk of being damaged.

Most spring frosts are ground frosts, which have more of a penetrating effect than that of the air frost. To understand how ground frost moves, picture water running down a slope. Frost will travel in a similar way to this. Therefore, never position your glasshouse containing indoor bonsai at the bottom of a slope where the frost may collect in a frost pocket.

Light

The light factor during the growing season is the most important ingredient in successfully growing bonsai, more so than temperature. Bonsai will tolerate a much wider temperature range, but the light factor needs to be kept at a constantly high level. The beginner must not confuse a high level of light with strong sunlight. In fact most bonsai prefer filtered light. Most

Fig 125 (b)   Serissa showing black leaves through lack of light – the tree was placed in too dark an area.

garden centres sell small light meters and I would advise you to invest in one before siting a bonsai.

Bonsai which are kept in poor light conditions show signs of leggy growth on their stems between one set of leaves and the next, and leaves turn yellow because the development of chlorophyll is restricted. The answer to the indoor bonsai's light problem is a grow light.

Grow lights are special lights which can be purchased from garden centres and some electrical stores. There are two shapes, a tube and a shape similar to a normal light bulb. The light bulb type comes with either a screw fitting or a bayonet fitting; however, it would be advisable to consult an electrician or the sales person on placement and safety factors before attempting to erect such a light system.

Temperature

Next to light, temperature is the second most important consideration in creating a healthy bonsai tree. Temperature controls the period of dormancy of the deciduous indoor bonsai and many problems such as poor growth, leggy growth and dull coloured foliage are caused when the deciduous indoor bonsai is kept at a constant temperature level throughout the year. This is partly due to the fact that the bonsai cannot take the rest period which it needs. Nature has built in a mechanism telling the bonsai to close down its manufacturing process and survive during certain conditions. When these conditions fail to develop, the bonsai's balance is thrown out.

Care should be taken with watering during the winter period, when temperatures fluctuate. Some indoor trees such as the pomegranate which under normal conditions would need watering every one or two days, may now only need watering every two to four days. However, the bonsai should under no circumstances be allowed to dry out.

Too high a temperature can be just as damaging as a low temperature. Problems such as heat canker will arise from high temperature

Fig 126   The grow light emits red and blue rays, helping the green chlorophyll in winter.

Fig 127   Dead myrtles – due to being placed in a living-room with too high a temperature.

and some of the cold room bonsai such as the olive will drop its leaves. Temperatures can be split into two – indoor bonsai and cold room bonsai.

Indoor Bonsai

The indoor bonsai are evergreen and deciduous, tropical and sub-tropical trees and shrubs. Both need a total frost-free growing condition with a temperature range between 15–21°C (59–70°F).

Cold Room Bonsai

Evergreen bonsai may be kept between 10–16°C (50–61°F) and deciduous bonsai to a temperature also between 10–16°C (50–61°F), but the temperature should be allowed to fall to 4°C (39°F) to allow the deciduous tree to enter a dormancy period, again with totally frost-free conditions.

CHAPTER 10

Month-by-Month Guide

JANUARY

January can be one of the coldest months of the year, and unlike the worry of over-wintering hardy bonsai, the problems of the indoor bonsai may be very confusing to the beginner.

As outdoor temperatures drop, indoor temperatures are raised by turning up the central heating. Warm air gas central heating presents itself as the first major problem which creates a warm, dry atmosphere around the foliage of the bonsai. This may lead to the bonsai taking on a dried, sick appearance. The leaves are affected by dust. Adding this to the low level of light and the rise and fall in day and night temperatures inside the house, the bonsai may go through several changes.

Changes may vary from sappy growth forming long sections between nodes, leaves turning yellow or black on the tips and sometimes dropping, to the tree refusing to give any form of new growth. In some cases the tree may also break forth with flowers. The reason for most of the above is the built-in time mechanism telling the tree when it should grow, when it should stop growing, and when to flower. This is the reason why when drawing your plan it is advisable to make notes on the type of tree, its temperature range, the light factor and when it flowers. In other words, research is very important when considering an indoor tree. Once you have found out all the information possible, try to create those conditions using grow lights, a humidity tray and in some cases creating an artificial environment such as the fish tank construction.

Placement

Never place your tree on top of the television. A grow light can be very useful if only dark positions are available; however, if there is a chance to place your tree in natural daylight, it can be very beneficial. In months such as January, the daylight is limited and therefore both natural and artificial light should be used to ensure sufficient levels.

The length of daylight required depends on the type of tree and the conditions under which it would grow naturally in its native country. Remember to remove the tree from the window position between the hours of about 6 p.m. and 7 a.m.

Placing the tree on a window with a radiator below is acceptable, providing the tree is not resting on direct heat and the temperature does not reach a higher level than is recommended for the type of tree being used. Rotating the tree each day is a worthwhile practice; this will encourage the tree to produce a balanced growth from the front, back and sides.

Other forms of heating such as radiators do not cause as many problems as warm air or gas central heating. The exception to this is a coal fire, and unless good ventilation and a dust-free atmosphere can be created, I would advise that the bonsai be kept in a well-lit, ventilated corner well away from the fire or in another room.

Watering/Misting

Always water with rain-water if possible, or boiled water that has been standing for more

Fig 128   An old fish tank will make an excellent display unit for indoor bonsai.

than twenty-four hours. Water from the top of the pot and not by standing in a bowl and watering by capillary action. Spraying the foliage with a fine mist spray will help to overcome the problem of dry atmosphere.

Humidity trays (dishes without holes which hold water) can be used, providing you follow the important rule of never allowing the base of the pot to be submerged in water for lengthy periods of time. Therefore, fill the tray with pebbles or use four small stones as pillars to stand the pot on. This allows water to drain through the holes in the bottom of the pot and air to enter.

Feeding

Continue to follow a feeding programme during this month, but remember to alternate between a balanced fertiliser containing N:P:K and trace elements, and tomato feed also containing some trace elements. Again, the important rule is not to over feed the bonsai.

Pest

Keep a check on your bonsai for pests such as red spider mite; examine the underside of the leaves as well as in the crowded areas of the branch-work for a fine webbing. As far as possible, remove any pests found by hand. If insecticide sprays are used, remember to use a bottle type rather than an aerosol. This will give you more control over the strength of the spray. It would be advisable to spray out of doors on a still day, but not in bright sunlight and always wash the container and your hands after spraying.

Diseases

Mainly trouble-free this time of year except for problems caused by bad pruning, lack of light, poor ventilation, too low or too high a temperature, over or under watering and over feeding. These symptoms show themselves as follows:

1   Bad pruning – die-back and rots.
2   Lack of light – black growing tips.
3   Poor ventilation – general unhealthy look.
4   Temperature/watering – mildews, wilting and rots.
5   Over feeding – wilting or too much sappy growth.

FEBRUARY

The month of February is almost the same as January for temperature and light conditions. This month should therefore be the rest period for the tree. By this I mean that the feeding programme at the end of this month will change to a balanced fertiliser containing more nitrogen. Root pruning can start, followed by a vigorous training programme throughout the coming year. Therefore, stop all feeding (for this month only) to allow any unused nutrients to become absorbed into the tree's system, stop all cosmetic pruning and let the tree grow unchecked

Fig 129   Chinese water elm seedling with sappy growth due to over feeding and poor light conditions.

for this month. Large branches may still be removed towards the end of the month.

Seed

Start looking for suppliers of indoor bonsai seed ready to sow at the end of the month. Unlike the hardy seed which can often be purchased at a garden centre or easily ordered, you may have to contact a seed specialist or bonsai nursery and place your order for seeds ready for the start of the sowing season over the next couple of months (*see* page 31).

Tools

During the quiet periods of this month, time should be spent on cleaning and repairing pruning tools, especially leaking sprayers. In most cases it will just be a washer or piece of pipe that is needed, but for those sprayers beyond repair I would suggest that you re-invest in a new one, preferably with a brass nozzle. Old sprayers will not only give you an uncontrollable jet or fine mist, but may also become a health risk to yourself through chemicals leaking on to your skin (another reason why you should always wear rubber gloves).

This month is also a good time for ordering new tools, especially those imported from Japan, because it is the time of year when most bonsai centres receive their orders of pots and tools ready for the new bonsai year.

Compost

Do not mix your compost until the end of this month, but at the same time it would be advisable to check with your garden centre when fresh supplies of materials will be arriving. As far as possible never buy last year's compost even though it may be on offer at a cut price. Always wait until their bargains have sold out and they have re-stocked with new supplies. Gravel, sand and grit, on the other hand, may be purchased from old or new stock.

Fig 130   Basic tools used for growing bonsai.

Chemicals

This is a good month to sit down and work out your spraying programme for the coming year. The same applies to chemicals as it does to compost and I have listed below a few tips:

1   Always wait until fresh stocks of chemicals reach the shelves. More damage may be caused if you try to save a few pence buying chemicals which are out of date. Therefore try to work out a programme which will allow a bottle or packet of chemical spray to last no longer than one year.
2   Never accept left-overs from friends, and always keep the chemical in its marked bottle or packet.
3   Try to estimate how much you will need for each spray, which will avoid having to find a safe way of disposing of unused chemicals.
4   Never empty chemicals into waterways and always keep them away from children and pets.

Root Pruning and Re-potting

Decide whether your tree will need root pruning and re-potting during the next two months, and if so choose your pot accordingly. At this time of year everybody is starting to think of re-potting their tree or trees, and suppliers of pots may find it hard to keep up with the demand. I

would suggest purchasing your pots at the earliest convenience otherwise you may be disappointed in not finding the right pot at the right time. It will be advisable if root pruning and re-potting to choose a pot either the same size or slightly larger. Never over-pot (this means to use a pot several times larger than the root ball).

Watering

Keep a check on watering and spray over the foliage in dry atmospheres. Refer to the list on indoor bonsai for the recommended temperatures for your tree during the winter.

Feeding

Stop feeding this month.

Pest and Disease

Check for pests and remove by hand if possible. Otherwise, spray for any disease problems that may be occurring. Some of the disease problems may be caused through too high or too low a temperature and bad ventilation. Therefore, again check the correct temperature for the tree and make sure there is adequate ventilation. Purchase new stocks of insecticide and fungicide sprays ready for the coming season.

MARCH

This month is probably the busiest of the year, with root pruning, re-potting and looking for insects which start to reveal themselves, seeking a sheltered host. Ideas start to suggest themselves on how new branches from the next stage of your plan will look, a new position indoors or a new area to be built outside ready for those long, warm sunny days when the indoor bonsai can take its prime position in the garden.

The spring frosts can still be a problem until the first two weeks of May, and therefore never be tempted to place your tree outside on the odd sunny day during the next two months, and move the tree away from the window during the night time.

Root Pruning and Re-Potting

I have found that this is the best month for root pruning and re-potting (*see* root pruning and re-potting, pages 47 to 49). Extra precautions to follow are to check the root ball for signs of pest or disease, and check that the compost smells sweet. If it should smell like, the bottom of a muddy pond then there have been problems with the drainage system. Therefore check further into the root system to make sure there are no rotting roots which could cause problems at a later stage.

Seed Sowing

If you have not already started, this is a good time to start seed sowing. Read the section on seed sowing, page 31 to 35.

Cutting

Provided you have some form of bottom-heat such as a propagator (with a thermostat control), start taking softwood cuttings (*see* page 36).

Watering

The general rule is to start increasing the watering (depending on the type of tree), and at the same time do not over water, especially those trees which have been root pruned. Continue to spray over the foliage if a humidity tray is not used, but remember not to submerge the bottom of the pot into water for long periods. As far as possible use rain water; if this is not available, use tap water that has been boiled and left to stand for twenty-four hours.

Feeding

Start using a balanced N:P:K feed plus trace elements, making sure it is the foliar feed type if the tree has been root pruned. The strength of the spray should be slightly under the recommended rate shown on the bottle or packet. Never over feed the tree. If the tree looks sick and you are following a feeding programme, look for the cause from elsewhere, such as insects or disease. Sometimes the tree may be shedding old, unwanted foliage; don't panic at the first sight of trouble, just follow your normal feeding, watering and spraying for pest and disease, making sure you have provided the correct temperature and light factors, but as a precaution isolate the tree from other bonsai.

Pest and Disease

Aphids and red spider mite will start to show themselves from this month onward. Therefore during the next two months keep a sharp surveillance over your bonsai by checking under the leaves as well as the top of them, and all the nooks and crannies along the branches and down the trunk. Also check for diseases such as powdery mildew, rots and die-back. Follow a spraying programme (*see* pest and disease section).

APRIL

In April most of your indoor trees should start producing an abundance of new growth, but do not dive head-on into pruning and shaping. Remember the bonsai has just spent several months being pushed between light and dark, and withstood many fluctuations in temperature. Therefore, by all means keep the tree under control, but allow it to take a rest and spread its branches this month.

Holidays

From April up to the end of September, watering is one of the top priorities of bonsai growing. To allow the bonsai to dry out will in most cases cause the death of the tree, so it is important that arrangements are made for watering your bonsai whilst you are away on holiday. Below I have divided the problems into short and long stay, to help overcome them.

Short Stay   These are periods between one to three days and for these short periods there is not always a need to call on neighbours, friends or relatives for help, although it is far better if you have somebody you can trust just in case your short holiday stay is unexpectedly extended for a few more days. Therefore the first people to approach are neighbours and friends.

First invite them round to see your bonsai collection, talk about it and show them how concerned you are for its upkeep. Explain the importance of watering, feeding and temperature. Offer them a small seedling if you have one. All this will go towards them taking an interest rather than considering it a chore to be carried out just because you are their neighbour/friend.

Although I said earlier, never water your tree by capillary action, there are the odd times of the year such as holidays when this may be the only form of watering the tree can receive. Most good garden centres will sell capillary matting, which looks like a normal mat made of wool. One end is placed under a source of water such as the tap in the bath or sink, the tap is turned on, but only allowed to drip. The moisture will impregnate the mat and be transported to the part where the pot is standing. A smaller piece or strip of the mat is pushed gently in to the drainage hole, and the bonsai is then watered by capillary action.

This technique is for short-period watering only and bonsai should not be watered this way normally, regardless of what some people may say. It is very important that the bonsai retains free drainage through the drainage hole and even more important that air is allowed to pass freely through the pot and compost.

Long Stay   During the summer months, most indoor bonsai can be placed outside for short periods and cold room bonsai for longer periods. One of the practices for hardy bonsai is to bury it in clean soil which is soaked with water, helping to keep the bonsai moist. However, because of the unpredictable weather in this country, this practice should only be carried out in a glasshouse when dealing with indoor bonsai. Cold room bonsai would probably tolerate a sudden drop in temperature, but less hardy trees would die from exposure, plus the fact that the occasional frost and even hailstones could still cause damage to the foliage even during the month of May. Therefore you are left with three options for indoor bonsai:

1   Contact your local bonsai nursery to find out if they offer a holiday care service.
2   Bury your bonsai in the soil of the glasshouse or cold frame which is then soaked the same way as you would for open ground. Leave a vent open to control high temperatures, and erect some shading.
3   For those without glasshouses make a trench and fill it with clean compost, bury your bonsai in its pot and soak the area. Then make a tent-like covering with sheets of plastic, or better still buy a ready-made piece of equipment normally used for vegetable growing and hope that the temperature does not drop too low.

Placement

Give the bonsai as much light as possible, but not direct sunlight. For those trees placed close to windows, remove them and position them inside the room away from the window during the night when temperatures may still drop below zero (*see* Frost, page 113). On warm, sunny days the tree can be placed outside, but allow the sun to warm the area first, or as a guide-line place it outside between the hours of 10 a.m. and 4 p.m. Try to avoid too much of a change in temperature, as this can be very harmful to the tree. If you are housebound and therefore unable to place a tree outside, try to give it as much ventilation as possible, but do not place it in a draft.

Watering

An increase in the watering is a normal practice at this time of year, but having said that there are no hard and fast rules, and it is therefore a case of temperature levels. By this I mean if the weather is cold, wet and cloudy outside this will affect the light factor and therefore the growing rate, which means the tree slows down its production factors and therefore too much water will do more harm than good. Remember always to use rain water if possible, or boiled water that has been standing for twenty-four hours.

Feeding

Continue to feed with a balanced fertiliser (*see* page 29) throughout this month and stick to your feeding programme without being tempted to over feed.

Pest

Most of the troublesome pests such as aphid, red spider mite and caterpillars start feeding and breeding, especially on warm sunny days when they come to life and move into conservatories and glasshouses. As far as possible remove them by hand, but at the same time stick to a preventative spraying programme (*see* Pests, pages 117 to 124).

Disease

Keep checking seeds for damping-off disease (*see* page 35). Other problems, such as die-back due to frost or previous bad pruning should be removed and the wound covered with a sealant containing a fungicide. If the tree is wilting, check for over or under watering and over feeding.

Propagation

Continue to take softwood cuttings.

Frost

Although in most cases the problem of frost will not affect the indoor bonsai (other than placing the tree too close to the window during the night), it would be advisable to read through the section on frost, page 113.

MAY

By the second week of May the bonsai should be showing signs of strong, healthy new growth. This is the time to start thinking about shaping. You should already have drawn a first and second dimensional plan showing when to stop the branch's growing tip and the position and direction in which the sub-lateral branches (side branches) will grow. The plan will need adding to as the tree grows, basically because of unforeseen events such as branches lost through damage, disease or pest.

Wiring

In most cases if the tree is deciduous, such as pomegranate, allow it to enter a dormant season (*see* Pomegranate, page 83). I would advise the beginner to make life easy and wire before the foliage is produced, but for evergreen types this is a good time to start. Remember – do not wire young, green growth; allow the bark to become woody, and always remove the wire six months later.

Watering

As for April.

Feeding

As for April.

Pest and Disease

Follow a spraying programme throughout the year.

Placement

On warm, sunny days it will help if the bonsai can be placed outside, but again if you are house-bound, give the tree as much ventilation as possible. Keep the tree indoors during the night this month.

Holidays

See April.

JUNE

June can be an unpredictable month, either full of rain or dry and hot, but the good aspect is that the spring frost should be over and therefore you can allow the indoor bonsai to remain outside for longer periods on warm days; but still remember to avoid direct sunlight. Continue to prune and shape, following your plan as far as possible.

Propagation

Semi-ripe cuttings can be taken this month (see page 36). The good thing about the semi-ripe cutting is that in most cases you can get away from using bottom-heat.

Watering

As for May.

Feeding

Change from the balanced feed of N:7 P:7 K:7 to a feed lower in nitrogen (N), but higher in phosphate (P) and potash (K). This will control and slow down the top growth, but at the same time benefit the root system of flowering bonsai and strengthen the new sappy growth. See Feeding, pages 24 to 27.

Pest and Disease

Follow a spraying programme throughout the year.

Placement

As for May, but on very warm nights you have the option of placing the semi-cold room bonsai outside.

Holidays

See April.

JULY

This month is basically the same as June, but extra care should be given against pests.

Watering

As for June.

Feeding

As for June.

Pest and Disease

Follow a spraying programme throughout the year, but pay extra attention to pests such as aphid and red spider mite.

Placement

As for June.

Holidays

See April.

AUGUST

This is generally the end of the summer for the indoor bonsai. By this I mean that temperatures may start to fall during the night, as do the day temperatures toward the end of the month. It therefore becomes too risky to place the indoor bonsai outside. The return to indoor conditions should, however, be gradual by first giving the tree as much light as possible, and a temperature similar to that of the temperature when placed outside.

Watering

Keep a check on watering, which can be one of the most important factors at this time of year. This is because due to the gradual drop in temperature, the light factor becoming less and then the confusion of placement with its fluctuation in both light and temperature, the tree's time clock is upset. In some cases a few of the leaves will change colour and drop, others will dry up and fall off, some trees start to flower and others will put on new growth. Therefore, to over water can do more harm than good and a balance between wet and dry must be found and maintained until the tree sorts itself out and returns to normality. Check drainage holes to ensure there is a good drainage still working.

Feeding

Again like the watering, the tree becomes confused, stopping and starting its manufacturing process. Therefore stick to a feeding programme and do not become tempted to over feed. At the end of the month you can start to alternate between a feed low in nitrogen one month then a tomato feed the next month. The high potash of the tomato feed will help the tree ripen its sappy wood and prepare it for winter.

Pest and Disease

Continue to spray throughout the year by sticking to a spraying programme. For those bonsai which have been placed outside, look for moths and other pests which may be starting to find overwintering positions.

Holidays

See April.

SEPTEMBER

As with the month of August the temperatures can be unpredictable and therefore it is too risky to place your bonsai outside. As the month draws to a close keep checking on those bonsai placed outside for pest who are either looking for a winter position or a host plant in warmer conditions. Again light and temperature will upset the tree's time clock and therefore the same applies to watering and feeding the tree as it did in August.

Watering

As for August.

Placement

As much light as possible, but not direct sunlight. Keep away from direct heat such as cookers, radiators and open fires and never place the tree over direct heat, such as the television. If the tree is placed on a window ledge with a radiator below, try to avoid siting the bonsai over the direct heat of the radiator.

Pest and Disease

As for August.

Holidays

See April.

OCTOBER

The autumn frost and low temperature should be the main concern for those people keeping indoor bonsai either in a conservatory or close to a window. For the conservatory it would be advisable to apply some form of heat which will control the inside temperature and keep out the frost. For a number of years in my own conservatory I have used a small electric fan heater with a thermostat control which has given me great success. For those keeping your bonsai close to a window follow the practice of moving the tree away from the window into a more central position in the room. Again allow for the tree to settle into the fluctuation of light and heat.

Pruning

Do not prune any tree that looks unwell due to movement, or from the change-over from summer light and temperature to winter light and temperature. For those bonsai which have acclimatised, continue to prune new, unwanted growth.

Wiring

Remove wire placed on the tree earlier in the year. See removing wire, page 45.

Watering

As for September.

Feeding

As for September.

Pest and Disease

Follow a spraying programme throughout the year.

Holidays

See April.

NOVEMBER

Basically the same as October, but your tree should have acclimatised itself to the indoor conditions. If not, try moving to a lighter or shadier spot, whichever the case may be, or a cooler or warmer position. This is a matter of trial and error until the ideal position is found.

Pruning

Continue to prune new, unwanted growth.

Watering

As for October.

Feeding

As for October.

Pest and Disease

As for October.

Holidays

See April.

Fig 131   Pomegranates in a group planting.

DECEMBER

At this time of year you should remember never to allow the bonsai to dry out, and never forget to feed it. Most of your local garden centres and large department stores start selling bonsai trees, but before you decide on a present for yourself or a loved one, read through Chapter 2 on buying a bonsai. After reading it remember there is nothing wrong in purchasing a tree from either the garden centre or the department store as most are supplied by good bonsai nurseries, but try as far as possible to get some form of help and an advice sheet or back-up service. Check for drainage, a root showing through the bottom of the pot, pots glazed on the inside and wire marks. Remember, the first bonsai is the most important one. If you lose the first tree you may lose interest in bonsai altogether.

Pruning

Continue to remove new, unwanted growth.

Watering

As for November.

Feeding

As for November.

Pest and Disease

As for October.

Holidays

See April.

Index